RELATIONSHIP BUILDING COMPASS

How to Communicate Effectively and Unleash a Healthy Connection

Rex Marcus

Copyright © 2024

Legal Notice

Disclaimer

Please note that the information contained in this book is for educational purposes only. The author and publisher have taken concerted efforts to present accurate and reliable information. No warranties of any kind are declared or implied. Readers acknowledge that the author is not engaging in the rending of legal, financial, medical, or professional advice. The content within this book has been derived from various reliable sources. By reading this document, the reader agrees that under no circumstances is the author responsible for any losses, direct or indirect, which are incurred as a result of the use of the information contained within this document, including, but not limited to, errors, omissions, or inaccuracies.

Relationship Building Compass: Table of Contents

Book 1: Effective Communication for Partners

BOOK 2: UNLEASHING HEALTHY RELATIONSHIPS

BOOK 1: EFFECTIVE COMMUNICATION FOR PARTNERS

How To Engage in Active Listening, De-Escalate Conflict and
Build Lasting Connection

Introduction

When it comes to love and relationships, the language we use isn't necessarily limited to words. It's a uniformity of emotions, gestures, movements, and unsaid wishes. Despite the greatest intentions, misunderstandings sometimes occur, leaving us feeling detached and irritated. The fact is that we all have different methods of giving and receiving love, and acknowledging these variations is the foundation for developing a meaningful and long-lasting relationship.

Cast your mind back to a period when you felt genuinely treasured by your lover. What caused you to feel so loved? Was it a sincere praise, a surprise present, a shared activity, or just the gift of their whole attention? Perhaps it was a blend of these, or something altogether new. The solution rests in comprehending love languages.

There are five major ways humans express and feel love: words of affirmation, acts of service, receiving gifts, quality time, and physical touch. Each of us has a dominant love language, which is frequently distinct from our partner's. This is where the magic occurs, but also where misinterpretation may occur.

Imagine pouring your heart into communicating love in your own tongue, only to have your spouse completely miss the point because they perceive love differently. Perhaps you lavish them with verbal compliments, but they seek meaningful time together. Perhaps you go out of your way to do things for them, yet they need physical attention. The goal is to learn and speak your partner's love language fluently.

This does not imply ignoring your own wants or interests. It's about accepting that what makes you feel loved may not be the same for your spouse. Recognizing and accepting these distinctions allows you to adjust your professions of love to fully connect with them, and vice versa.

Understanding your couple's communication style is just as important as knowing their love languages. Is your communication style more direct or indirect? Are you a good listener, or do you struggle to understand what your spouse is saying? How do you manage conflict? Do you attempt to fix it right away, or do you need time to process your feelings first?

These are just a few of the questions you may ask each other to better understand how you interact as a couple. By evaluating your own strengths and shortcomings, you may create techniques for speaking more effectively, resolving problems constructively, and developing a deeper, more personal relationship.

Chapter 1: Building a Strong Foundation for Love

For every timeless love tale, whether told through the centuries or unfolding in the current moment, is founded on a set of key characteristics. These ingredients, like the solid beams and mortar of a well-built home, give the structure and support required to weather life's storms and create a refuge of warmth, connection, and long-term enjoyment.

At the center of this foundation is trust, a valuable and fragile gift that must be gained and cultivated over time. Trust is the notion that your spouse has your best interests in mind, that they will be honest and loyal, and that they will always have your back, no matter what. It is the courage to be vulnerable, to reveal your innermost fears and hopes, knowing that you will not be criticized or mocked.

Without trust, a relationship is like a building constructed on shifting sand, prone to collapse at the least earthquake. Building trust requires time, effort, and consistent delivery on commitments. It requires open and honest communication, openness, and the ability to recognize errors and apologize as needed.

Respect goes hand in hand with trust, indicating a deep understanding for your partner's uniqueness, ideas, and limits. Respect entails appreciating others' viewpoints, even if they vary from your own. It entails respecting their autonomy, providing them freedom to be themselves, and promoting their own development and goals.

Disrespect, on the other hand, has the potential to destroy a relationship's basis like acid on stone. It might take the form of criticism, belittlement, sarcasm, or downright disdain. A lack of respect may cause deep scars that are difficult to repair, eventually driving a chasm between two individuals who previously loved one other dearly.

Shared values are another critical component in creating a solid foundation for love. While it is not essential to agree on everything, having a basic agreement on core principles fosters a feeling of community and purpose. Shared values might range from religious or spiritual convictions to political opinions, social causes, or lifestyle choices.

When couples have a shared vision for the future, they are more likely to collaborate on mutual objectives, support each other's aspirations, and build a life that is meaningful and gratifying for both of them. Of all, disputes are unavoidable, and good ones may even spur intellectual and emotional development. However, when underlying beliefs are fundamentally mismatched, it may result in continual conflict and a feeling of detachment.

Emotional connection is the glue that holds all of the other pieces together. It is the experience of being profoundly seen, heard, and understood by your spouse. It is the capacity to express your pleasures and sorrows, hopes and anxieties, without judgment or hesitation. Open and honest communication, empathy, active listening, and the willingness to be vulnerable all help to establish emotional connection.

In a society that constantly bombards us with diversions and shallow relationships, emotional connection is a valuable and scarce asset. It's the warmth that comes from a shared look, the comfort of a loving hug, and the laughter that results from an inside joke. It's the sense of knowing you're not alone, that you have a companion who recognizes and loves you for who you are.

Truly Hearing Your Partner

Active listening goes beyond mere hearing and becomes a profound act of understanding, validation, and empathy. When you truly listen to your partner, you provide a safe environment for them to express their thoughts, feelings, and needs without fear of being judged or dismissed.

Consider a scenario in which your partner shares a story from their day. Are you totally engaged, absorbing their words and the subtle subtleties in their voice? Or are you absorbed with your own ideas, preparing a response before they are done speaking? Active listening entails directing your whole attention to your companion, both vocally and nonverbally. It entails pushing aside distractions, keeping eye contact, and making affirmative nods or movements to demonstrate that you are attentive.

However, attentive listening extends beyond merely being there. It demands you to pay attention to the emotional undercurrents behind your partner's remarks. Are they delighted, furious, frightened, or hopeful? Take note of their body language, facial expressions, and tone of speech. These nonverbal clues often convey more than words do.

After you've comprehended the emotional depth of your partner's communication, think on what you've heard. Summarize their main points, acknowledge their feelings, and validate their experience. This not only ensures that you've understood them correctly, but it also demonstrates your empathy and genuine interest in what they have to say.

Avoid interrupting or offering unsolicited advice. Instead, ask open-ended questions that encourage your partner to elaborate and delve deeper into their thoughts and feelings. This demonstrates that you appreciate their opinion and seek to understand them on a deeper level.

Know that active listening is a two-way street. Just as you want to be heard and understood by your spouse, they seek the same from you. When both couples practice active listening, it generates a virtuous circle of connection and intimacy.

By practicing active listening abilities, you may convert your interactions into chances for greater connection and understanding. You can improve dispute resolution, enhance emotional bonds, and establish a partnership built on mutual respect and support.

Consider the effect of active listening in several situations: when your spouse discusses a personal accomplishment, an unpleasant professional experience, or a weakness that they haven't revealed with anyone else. The capacity to fully listen and react with empathy may make a significant impact in how people feel heard, appreciated, and loved.

Nurturing Emotional Intimacy

Appreciation and gratitude are powerful currencies in the terrain of love. It is the lifeblood that sustains the emotional connection between lovers, reinforcing the links that bind them together. Like sunshine to a budding flower, expressing appreciation and gratitude exposes the depths of a relationship, creating an atmosphere in which love may develop and thrive.

Remember the last time your spouse did anything to make you smile, feel cherished, or brighten your day. Did you tell them how much it meant to you? Have you expressed your genuine gratitude? While the act may seem little, recognizing it may have a significant influence on the emotional landscape of your relationship.

When we show thankfulness, we not only recognize our partner's efforts, but we also send a deeper message of love and appreciation. It's a way of expressing, "I see you, I value you, and I appreciate how you enrich my life." These remarks, whether said or unspoken, create a positive feedback loop that encourages good actions and enhances the emotional bond between couples.

What about a situation in which your spouse goes out of their way to make your favorite dinner after a hard day? How did you react to that? Expressing your thanks, whether with a genuine "thank you" or a warm hug, shows them that their efforts were acknowledged and appreciated. This simple act of acknowledgment stimulates their desire to continue doing the things that make you happy, resulting in a circle of mutual appreciation and affection.

The beauty of expressing appreciation and thanks is that it can be done in so many different ways. It does not necessarily have to include large gestures or extravagant demonstrations. Sometimes the most powerful phrases are the simplest. A handwritten note left on the bathroom mirror, a surprise cup of coffee in bed, or a text message expressing your love and gratitude may all make a big difference.

Words of affirmation are effective ways to convey thanks. Telling your spouse how much you love and respect them, emphasizing certain characteristics or behaviors you enjoy, or just reminding them of their significance in your life may all help to strengthen your emotional connection. Be honest, detailed, and passionate in your remarks, and see how your partner's face lights up with excitement and gratitude.

Acts of service are another way to express thanks. Being nice to your spouse without being asked communicates your love and concern in a practical manner. It might be as easy as cooking them breakfast in bed, doing a duty they loathe, or providing a massage after a long day. The goal is to do something you know your spouse would like, and to do it with love and generosity.

Physical contact is a global language of love and may be an effective means of expressing thanks. A warm embrace, a delicate caress, or a long kiss may convey so much without saying anything. Physical affection causes the production of oxytocin, known as the "love hormone," which promotes emotions of intimacy, trust, and connection. Make time for physical intimacy in your relationship, whether it's snuggling on the sofa, strolling together, or just providing a reassuring touch when your spouse is feeling low.

Gifts, great and little, may be powerful demonstrations of appreciation. The care and meaning behind the present are more important than its monetary worth. A present that matches your partner's interests, hobbies, or personal preferences demonstrates that you are paying attention to what is important to them. It may be a book by their favorite author, tickets to a concert they've been dying to attend, or a small item that reminds them of a particular time you had together.

Puzzle Exercise

Instruction:

Find the hidden words in the puzzle. Words can be written horizontally, vertically, or diagonally, forward or backward. Circle each word you find.

At the end of your attempt, look into the completed puzzle table to find out how correct you are.

BUILDING BLOCKS OF A HEALTHY AND FULFILLING RELATIONSHIP

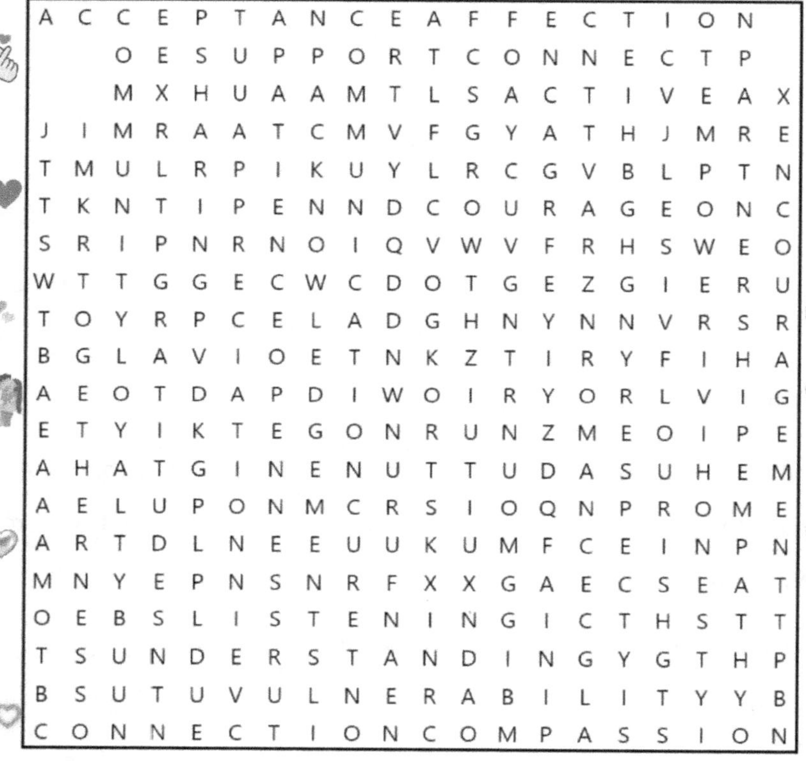

Acceptance	Growth	Respect
Acknowledgement	Honesty	Romance
Active listening	Intimacy	Security
Affection	Kindness	Sharing
Appreciation	Love	Support
Communication	Loyalty	Time
Connection	Nurturing	Togetherness
Empathy	Openness	Trust
Encouragement	Partnership	Understanding
Gratitude	Patience	Vulnerability

BUILDING BLOCKS OF A HEALTHY AND FULFILLING RELATIONSHIP

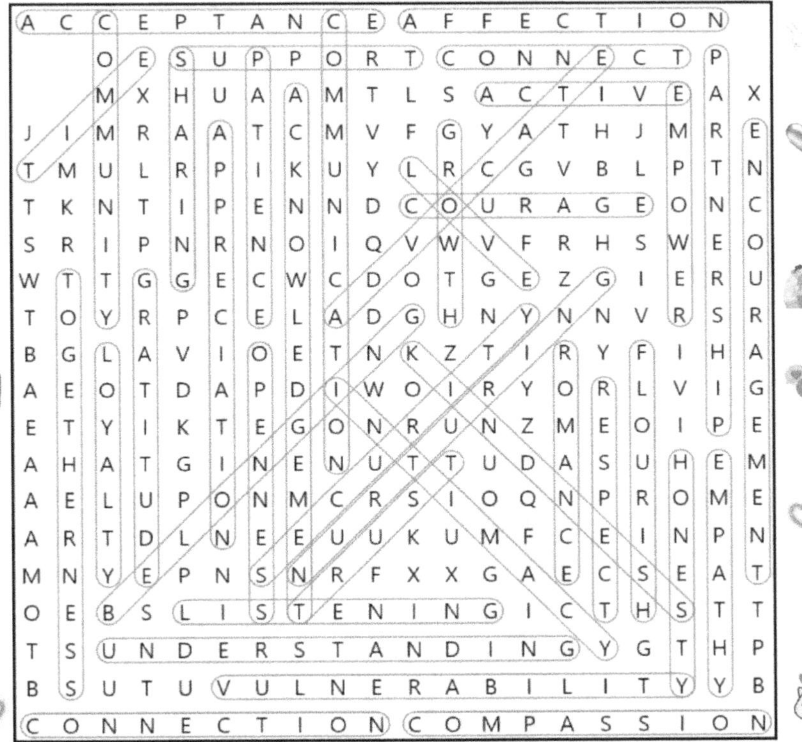

Acceptance	Growth	Respect
Acknowledgement	Honesty	Romance
Active listening	Intimacy	Security
Affection	Kindness	Sharing
Appreciation	Love	Support
Communication	Loyalty	Time
Connection	Nurturing	Togetherness
Empathy	Openness	Trust
Encouragement	Partnership	Understanding
Gratitude	Patience	Vulnerability

Chapter 2: Navigating Conflict with Love and Respect

Disagreements are a normal aspect of every relationship. However, just as a gentle rain may nurture, a heavy deluge can be destructive. The key to dealing with conflict in a relationship is not to avoid it completely, but to approach it with love, respect, and a desire to find solutions that benefit both parties.

You might want to remember situations in which you and your spouse have opposing views about how to spend your weekend. You may anticipate a nice night in, but they need adventure and excitement. Instead of digging in your heels and insisting on your own route, approach the problem with openness and empathy. To better comprehend their point of view, use open-ended questions such as, "What sounds fun to you this weekend?" What do you want to gain out of it?

By really listening to their wishes and needs, you may realize that their concept of adventure is a simple ramble in the woods or a trip to a new neighborhood you've never visited together. Alternatively, they may be prepared to make a compromise and agree to a relaxing night in followed by a spontaneous adventure the following day.

The key is to see conflict as a collaborative problem-solving exercise, rather than a struggle to be won or lost. This necessitates a change in perspective from "me versus you" to "us against the problem." When both partners feel heard and understood, they are more willing to consider innovative solutions that suit everyone's requirements.

Recognizing and controlling one's own emotions is a crucial element of successful conflict resolution. When we are angry, upset, or irritated, we tend to lash out or retreat. Take a minute to stop, breathe, and express your feelings without judgment. If necessary, take a break from the discussion until you feel calmer and more focused.

After you've had some time to calm down, you may rejoin the debate with a clearer brain and a more helpful attitude. Use "I" phrases to convey your emotions and demands without criticizing or condemning your spouse. For example, instead of stating, "You always ignore my feelings," try expressing, "I get hurt when I don't feel heard."

Concentrate on the current problem rather than bringing up old concerns. Avoid generalizations like "you always" or "you never," and instead describe the conduct that is hurting you. For example, instead of stating, "You never help around the house," say, "I would appreciate it if you could help me with the dishes tonight."

Remember that the purpose of dispute resolution isn't to prove who is right or wrong, but to find a solution that works for all parties. Be ready to compromise, let go of your ego, and put your relationship ahead of your own demands.

Despite your best efforts, confrontations may sometimes grow into furious fights. If this occurs, take a break from the talk and agree to resume it later when you're both more relaxed. Avoid raising your voice, calling them names, or making personal assaults. Remember that you're all on the same team, and the aim is to get a resolution.

If you are unable to settle disputes on your own, do not hesitate to seek the assistance of a couple's therapist or counselor. A qualified expert may provide advice and support as you build healthy communication skills and conflict resolution tactics.

Fair Fighting Rules

Disagreements are not hurdles on the path to love; rather, they may lead to greater understanding and connection. To prevent these diversions from becoming dead ends, developing a set of "fair fighting rules" might turn disagreements into chances for progress.

First and foremost, select your conflicts carefully. Not every dispute requires a full-fledged conversation. Some difficulties are modest and may be handled with a simple compromise or a shift in viewpoint. Save your energy for things that are genuinely important, like your basic principles, well-being, or the future of your partnership.

Timing is everything. If emotions are running high, it's frequently better to take a pause and return to the talk after you've both had a chance to calm down. This does not involve ignoring the matter; rather, it means scheduling the conversation for a time when both of you can approach it with clearer thoughts and calmer emotions.

When you have a debate, remember that the purpose is to understand, not to win. Listen to your partner's point of view, even if you disagree with it. Try to understand their underlying feelings and wants. Often, what seems to be a quarrel about a single subject is really the result of underlying worries, insecurities, or unfulfilled needs.

Express your own emotions and needs clearly and honestly, using "I" phrases to avoid blaming and accusations. Instead of stating, "You're always so insensitive," say, "I'm hurt when you dismiss my feelings." This approach encourages understanding rather than defensiveness.

Focus on the particular topic at hand rather than making broad generalizations. Instead of stating, "You never listen to me," add, "I felt unheard when I expressed my concerns about our finances." Be clear and direct in your message, and avoid bringing up previous issues.

Remember that compromise is not a sign of weakness, but of strength. It demonstrates that you appreciate your connection and are prepared to work together to find solutions that benefit both parties. This might imply meeting in the middle or taking turns getting your way. The trick is to remain adaptable and open to new options.

Above all, respect your spouse, even if you disagree. Avoid name-calling, insults, and personal assaults. Remember that you care about this individual, and your words have the ability to harm or heal. Choose love and compassion, even in the heat of the moment.

Finding Win-Win Solutions Together

Disagreements are not hurdles on the voyage of love; they are diversions that allow you to explore new pathways together. Instead of perceiving conflict as a war, consider it a dance - a precise choreography in which both partners move in unison, finding a beat that speaks to both hearts.

Compromise and cooperation are the steps that lead this dance. They are the skills that enable you to negotiate arguments with grace, compassion, and a shared commitment to finding solutions that respect both your individual needs and the health of your partnership.

Compromise does not mean surrendering your happiness or settling for less. It's about understanding that in every relationship, there will be moments when you must meet your spouse halfway. It's about finding a medium ground that meets both of your wants, even if it means giving up some of your choices.

Think about the weekend situation we outlined previously. Perhaps you had planned a calm night at home, but your companion was anxious for an adventure. Open communication and a readiness to compromise may reveal a mutual interest in exploring a new area or trying a new restaurant. This compromise not only fulfills both of your wants, but it also produces a unique shared experience, which improves your relationship.

Collaboration takes compromise one step further. It is about collaborating to develop innovative solutions that go beyond merely meeting in the middle. It's about brainstorming ideas, examining options, and devising a strategy that excites and satisfies both of you.

Imagine you and your lover are arranging a trip. Instead of bickering over whether to go to the beach or the mountains, work together to plan a vacation that includes both. Perhaps you'll spend a few days climbing in the mountains before resting on the beach. Or maybe you discover a resort that provides both outdoor activities and cultural encounters.

Open and honest communication is essential for compromise and cooperation. Express your demands and goals clearly, but also be open to hearing your partner's viewpoint. Be flexible, adaptive, and open to different options. Remember that you're working toward a similar goal: finding a solution that will make both of you happy and deepen your relationship.

When you approach conflict with the attitude of compromise and cooperation, you may turn it into an opportunity for development and connection. You learn more about each other's needs and preferences, improve your problem-solving abilities, and establish a greater feeling of trust and closeness. Finally, you develop a relationship in which both parties feel respected, heard, and loved.

Puzzle Exercise

Instruction:

Find the hidden words in the puzzle. Words can be written horizontally, vertically, or diagonally, forward or backward. Circle each word you find.

At the end of your attempt, look into the completed puzzle table to find out how correct you are.

MAINTAINING LOVE AND RESPECT

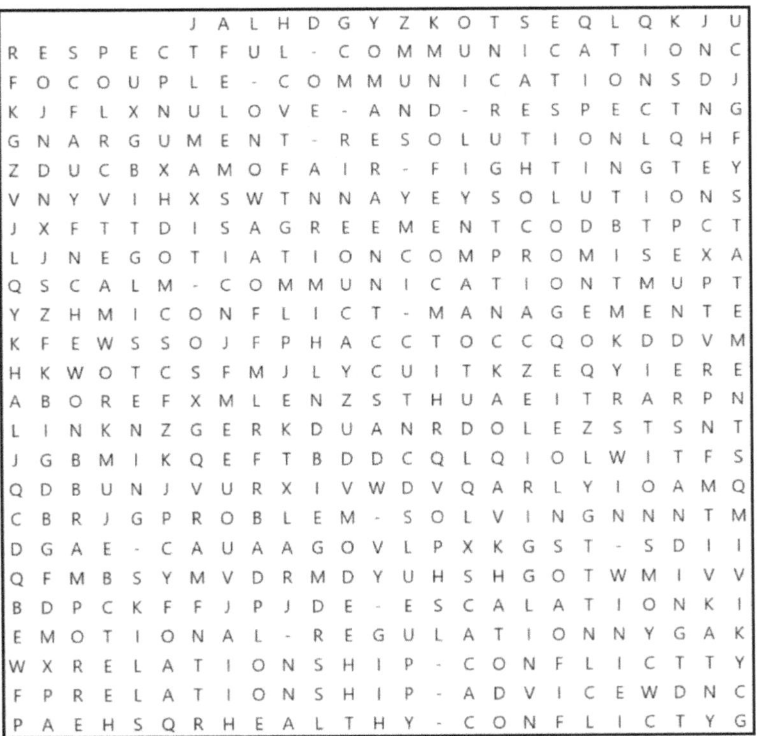

Argument-resolution	Healthy-conflict	Relationship skills
Calm-communication	Statements	Respectful-communication
Compromise	Listening-skills	
Conflict-management	Love-and-respect	Solutions
Couple-communication	Mediation	Teamwork
De-escalation	Negotiation	Understanding
Disagreement	Problem-solving	Validation
Emotional-regulation	Relationship-advice	Win-win
Fair-fighting	Relationship-conflict	

MAINTAINING LOVE AND RESPECT

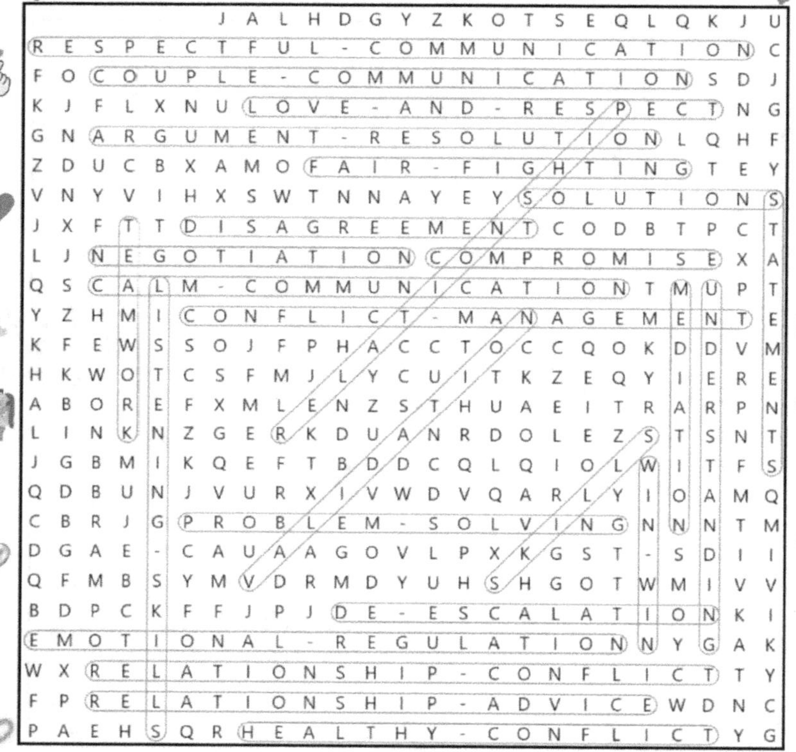

Argument-resolution	Healthy-conflict	Relationship skills
Calm-communication	Statements	Respectful-communication
Compromise	Listening-skills	
Conflict-management	Love-and-respect	Solutions
Couple-communication	Mediation	Teamwork
De-escalation	Negotiation	Understanding
Disagreement	Problem-solving	Validation
Emotional-regulation	Relationship-advice	Win-win
Fair-fighting	Relationship-conflict	

Chapter 3: Intimacy and Connection Beyond Words

In the world of love and intimacy, words are just one brushstroke in a rich image of connection. Beyond the spoken language, there exists nonverbal signs - delicate gestures, transient emotions, and unspoken desires. These nonverbal cues, which are sometimes misunderstood or undervalued, have enormous ability to enhance intimacy, rekindle love, and generate a profound feeling of connection among couples.

For example, a couple enjoying a candlelight meal. As they talk, their eyes meet and sparkle with unsaid feelings. A light touch on the arm, a knowing grin, a discreet lean-in—these apparently little actions express volumes, indicating love, desire, and a shared understanding that goes beyond words. Intimacy blooms best in these wordless moments of connection.

Body language is a global language of love that is expressed via the tilt of the head, the arch of the brow, or the soft brush of fingers. A loving hug may alleviate tension and anxiety, whilst a playful touch might inspire feelings of desire. Holding hands while strolling, snuggling on the sofa, or just providing a reassuring touch at a tough moment may all express feelings of love, support, and belonging.

Touch's power stems from its capacity to convey feelings that words cannot always portray. A delicate caress may offer compassion and love, whilst a forceful embrace might communicate power and stability. Physical contact produces oxytocin, the "love hormone," which promotes emotions of intimacy, trust, and connection. By putting physical contact first in your relationship, you create a safe haven in which both parties feel loved, valued, and intimately connected.

Facial expressions are another effective means of nonverbal communication. A genuine grin can brighten a room and warm a heart, yet a furrowed brow indicates stress or concern. Eye contact, sometimes known as the "windows to the soul," may express a variety of emotions, including love and admiration, despair, and rage. Paying attention to your partner's facial expressions provides vital information into their inner world and emotional condition.

Tone of voice is sometimes disregarded as a type of nonverbal communication, despite its importance in communicating meaning and emotion. A soft tone may soothe and comfort, but a strong tone can hurt and alienate. The tone of your voice, the tempo of your speaking, and the volume with which you speak all have an impact on how your message is perceived. By being aware of your tone of voice, you may guarantee that your words are in line with your objectives and that your partner feels heard and understood.

Beyond body language, touch, facial emotions, and tone of voice, there are several additional nonverbal indicators that influence how we communicate with loved ones. Dressing, decorating our houses, giving presents, and even sharing meals may all convey signals of love, caring, and gratitude.

By being more aware of these nonverbal indicators in yourself and your spouse, you may achieve a higher degree of intimacy and connection in your relationship. Pay attention to the subtle cues your spouse gives with their body language, touch, facial expressions, and tone of voice. Observe how people respond to your nonverbal clues and change your conversation appropriately.

Nonverbal Communication in Love

Body language, facial expressions, and subtle movements from your spouse may disclose a plethora of information about their feelings, wants, and desires in the unwritten language of love. Learning to recognize these nonverbal signs is like to unlocking a hidden code that helps you to connect with your spouse on a deeper, more intuitive level.

Imagine your lover sitting across from you at the dinner table. When you attempt to establish eye contact with them, they droop their shoulders, wrinkle their forehead, and their eyes flit away. You can tell there's something wrong even if no one says anything. Perhaps they are agitated, anxious, or just having a lousy day. By recognizing these nonverbal indicators, you may modify your approach and provide support and understanding.

Imagine your spouse grinning at you, their eyes gleaming with delight, and their body bending toward you. Their open posture and easy manner indicate that they are happy, pleased, and connected with you. This nonverbal feedback strengthens your relationship and promotes more pleasant encounters.

Learning how to interpret your partner's nonverbal clues is a continuous process that involves both observation and intuition. Take note of their facial expressions, body language, and tone of speech. Examine how they respond to various settings, discussions, and physical touches. Are they more inclined to open up when you sit beside them, or do they prefer face-to-face interactions? Do they react well to mild contact, or would they prefer more space?

As you become more aware of your partner's nonverbal clues, you will begin to recognize patterns and subtleties that reflect their inner world. You'll learn how to anticipate their needs, comprehend their feelings, and react in ways that deepen your relationship. For example, if you see that your spouse withdraws when they are overwhelmed, you may give them space and support without interfering or pushing.

Reading nonverbal clues also entails observing your own body language and how it impacts your partner. If you're worried or nervous, your spouse may pick up on the signals and replicate your feelings. Being aware of your own nonverbal signals allows you to communicate more effectively and foster a more pleasant and caring environment.

Nonverbal communication is a two-way street. Just as you learn to interpret your partner's unspoken indications, they are likewise monitoring yours. By being aware of your own body language, facial expressions, and tone of voice, you may convey your love, affection, and support in a manner that is genuinely meaningful to your spouse.

Physical Touch and Affection

In the language of love, touch is a dialect that talks straight to the heart. A single touch, a soft caress, or a warm hug may speak volumes, overcoming the limits of language and penetrating deep into our inner core. It's a language that is primordial, instinctual, and profoundly embedded in our human nature.

Consider the sensation of your partner's hand in yours as you walk through the park, the warmth of their hug when you have a peaceful time together, or the comfort of their touch as you fall asleep. These apparently modest actions have enormous ability to enhance your link, improve your closeness, and provide a feeling of safety and security in your relationship.

Physical contact produces oxytocin, sometimes known as the "love hormone," which promotes emotions of intimacy, trust, and connection. It relieves stress, lowers blood pressure, and even strengthens the immune system. When we touch our loved ones, we are not only showing affection, but also offering a concrete kind of emotional support and comfort.

The beauty of touch is that it can be conveyed in so many different ways. It's not always necessary to be overly amorous or sexual. A simple embrace when your spouse returns home from work, a lighthearted tickle after a shared laugh, or a soft touch on the arm during a chat may all express feelings of love, caring, and connection.

Some people's main love language is touch, which is how they feel most loved and valued. For others, it may be a second language, yet it remains a crucial means to communicate and receive love. Regardless of your love language, putting physical contact first in your relationship may have a significant influence on emotional intimacy and overall connection.

Schedule time for physical closeness in your everyday routine. Begin the day with a warm hug, hold hands while watching a movie, or snuggle before bedtime. Explore various sorts of touch, such as soft caresses, amusing tickles, and passionate kisses. Experiment with what works best for both of you, and don't be hesitant to express your wishes and preferences honestly.

Puzzle Exercise

Instruction:

Find the hidden words in the puzzle. Words can be written horizontally, vertically, or diagonally, forward or backward. Circle each word you find.

At the end of your attempt, look into the completed puzzle table to find out how correct you are.

NON-VERBAL COMMUNICATION

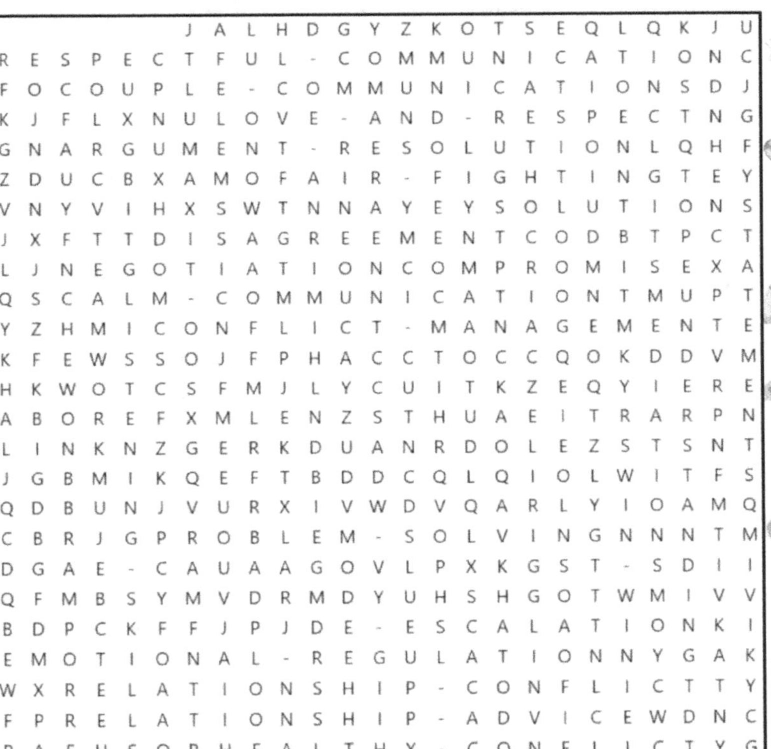

Affection	Love-language
Body language	Nonverbal-communication
Bonding	Physical-touch
Closeness	Romance
Communication-cues	Sensory-connection
Emotional-connection	Silent-communication
Eye-contact	Tactile-communication
Facial-expressions	Tone-of-voice
Intimacy	Touch
	Unspoken-language
	Wordless-communication

NON-VERBAL COMMUNICATION

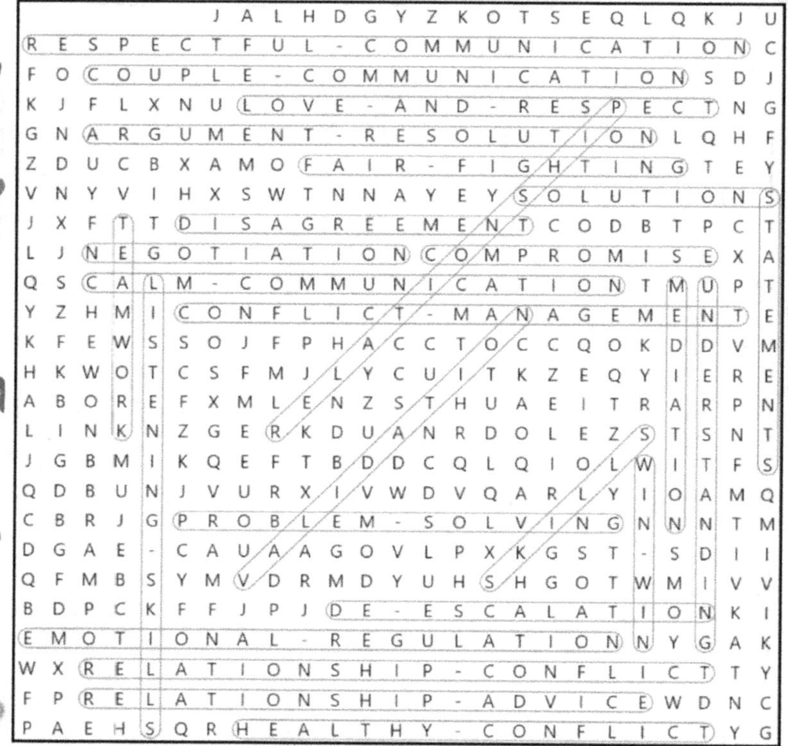

Affection

Body language

Bonding

Closeness

Communication-cues

Emotional-connection

Eye-contact

Facial-expressions

Intimacy

Love-language

Nonverbal-communication

Physical-touch

Romance

Sensory-connection

Silent-communication

Tactile-communication

Tone-of-voice

Touch

Unspoken-language

Wordless-communication

Chapter 4: Talking About the Tough Stuff

A love relationship brings together pleasure, laughter, and shared dreams. However, interlaced amid these vivid colors are fragile threads that symbolize the "tough stuff" - the sensitive themes that may cause conflicts, create worries, and shake the very basis of your relationship.

While it may be tempting to avoid these talks completely, doing so simply fosters anger and latent tensions. The key to a healthy and happy relationship is to approach these challenging matters with openness, honesty, and a shared commitment to understanding.

Money often tops the list of difficult topics for couples. Disagreements about spending patterns, financial objectives, or even the mere process of budgeting may rapidly turn into passionate debates. However, by approaching these talks with a shared desire to establish common ground, financial discussions may be transformed into opportunities for cooperation and progress.

Begin by creating up specific time to discuss money. Choose a time when you're comfortable and free of interruptions. Begin by understanding that money may be a touchy issue, and emphasize your willingness to collaborate to develop solutions that benefit both of you.

Share your distinct ideas about money. Do you prefer to save or spend? What are your financial objectives, both short and long term? Understanding each other's beliefs and priorities can help you bridge the gap between your financial strategies.

Make a common budget that represents both of your needs and objectives. This may need some compromise and discussion, but the idea is to find a solution that seems fair and reasonable to both of you. Regularly evaluate and change your budget as appropriate, and celebrate your accomplishments together.

Sex and intimacy are also difficult issues for many couples. Disagreements about frequency, preferences, and wants may result in emotions of rejection, frustration, and even humiliation. However, by encouraging open and honest discussion about sex, you may enhance your closeness and build a more rewarding sexual relationship.

Create a comfortable environment for frank discussion about sex. Begin by noting that this may be a sensitive subject, and express your wish to establish an environment in which both of you feel comfortable discussing your views and emotions without fear of being judged.

Share your dreams, wants, and worries. Be honest about your likes and dislikes, and urge your spouse to do the same. Remember, there is no right or wrong way to have pleasure; the most important thing is to discover what works best for both of you.

Experiment and discover together. Be open to new experiences and don't be scared to move outside of your comfort zone. The idea is to approach sexual exploration with a feeling of fun and curiosity.

Personal objectives are another crucial issue to discuss in a partnership. Your own desires, objectives, and ambitions influence who you are and what you want from life. Sharing your objectives with your spouse invites them into your inner world and fosters a stronger bond.

Make time to discuss your aspirations and objectives. Share your goals for the future, both personally and professionally. Discuss the measures you're doing to reach your objectives, and seek your partner's support and encouragement.

Celebrate each other's accomplishment. Be your partner's greatest cheerleader whenever they accomplish a goal, no matter how large or little. Your excitement and encouragement will not only enhance your friendship, but also motivate them to pursue their aspirations.

Communicating Openly About Finances

In every relationship, money often disguises itself as a simple issue of numbers and statistics. However, behind the surface, it contains a significant emotional charge, interwoven with our beliefs, aspirations, and worries. It's a subject that may elicit both excitement and stress, and how we talk about it can either build or sever our relationship.

Open and honest financial communication is vital for a successful and long-lasting partnership. When couples avoid or minimize money talks, it may lead to misunderstandings, anger, and even financial adultery. Open communication about money fosters trust and transparency, ensuring that both partners feel heard, appreciated, and empowered to make healthy financial choices together.

Begin by understanding that money may be a touchy issue. Share your own financial experiences and opinions. Did you grow up in a family where money was freely addressed, or was it a taboo subject? What are your financial objectives, both as individuals and couples?

Understanding each other's opinions and experiences can help you bridge the gap between your various financial approaches.

Set up frequent money dates to openly discuss your financial condition, aspirations, and concerns. Choose a moment when you are both comfortable and distraction-free. Create an agenda for the talk and avoid bringing up any sensitive issues that might derail it.

Make a common budget that represents both your needs and ideals. This may need some compromise and discussion, but the idea is to find a solution that seems fair and reasonable to both of you. Keep track of your expenditures, evaluate your budget on a regular basis, and celebrate your victories together.

Be open about your financial practices. If you have a propensity to overspend or amass debt, be honest with your spouse. Together, you can devise a strategy to overcome these obstacles and adopt healthy financial habits.

Sex and Intimacy

In the sphere of love, sex and intimacy are not only physical activities, but also powerful expressions of emotional connection. They are the whispers of yearning, wordless longings, and shared vulnerability that connect two souls. Sexual intimacy, when fostered with love and respect, has the potential to provide both parties with enormous pleasure, profound connection, and long-term contentment.

However, the route to sexual happiness is not always straightforward. Mismatched wants, unsaid expectations, and fear of vulnerability may all be impediments to honest communication and the formation of a really meaningful sexual relationship. The key to realizing this potential is creating an atmosphere in which both partners feel secure, heard, and empowered to communicate their wants and goals freely and honestly.

For example, a couple that has been together for many years. Their sexual needs and preferences may have changed over time, but they haven't disclosed them to one another. This lack of communication may cause irritation, anger, and a progressive decrease in sexual enjoyment. They may regain their passion and have a more rewarding sexual experience by fostering an open discourse about sex.

Begin by selecting a time and location where you both feel calm and comfortable. Turn off your phones and lower the lights to create an aura of closeness and openness. Begin by expressing your gratitude to your spouse and your wish to strengthen your sexual connection.

Share your dreams, wants, and tastes. Use detailed and descriptive terminology that both of you feel comfortable with. Avoid criticism or judgment, and instead convey your own needs and desires.

Encourage your spouse to do the same, and attentively listen to their comments while showing empathy and compassion.

Remember that honest discussion about sex is a continuous process. Your wants and tastes may vary over time, so maintain the lines of communication open as your relationship progresses. Check in with each other on a regular basis about your sexual wants and desires, and be open to trying new things together.

Creating a satisfying sexual relationship is more than just talking about sex. It is also about developing closeness and connection in other aspects of your relationship. Spend meaningful time together, express your love and admiration often, and emphasize physical intimacy. By cultivating a deep emotional connection, you create a conducive environment for sexual closeness to thrive.

Puzzle Exercise

Instruction:

Find the hidden words in the puzzle. Words can be written horizontally, vertically, or diagonally, forward or backward. Circle each word you find.

At the end of your attempt, look into the completed puzzle table to find out how correct you are.

ADDRESSING CHALLENGING TOPICS

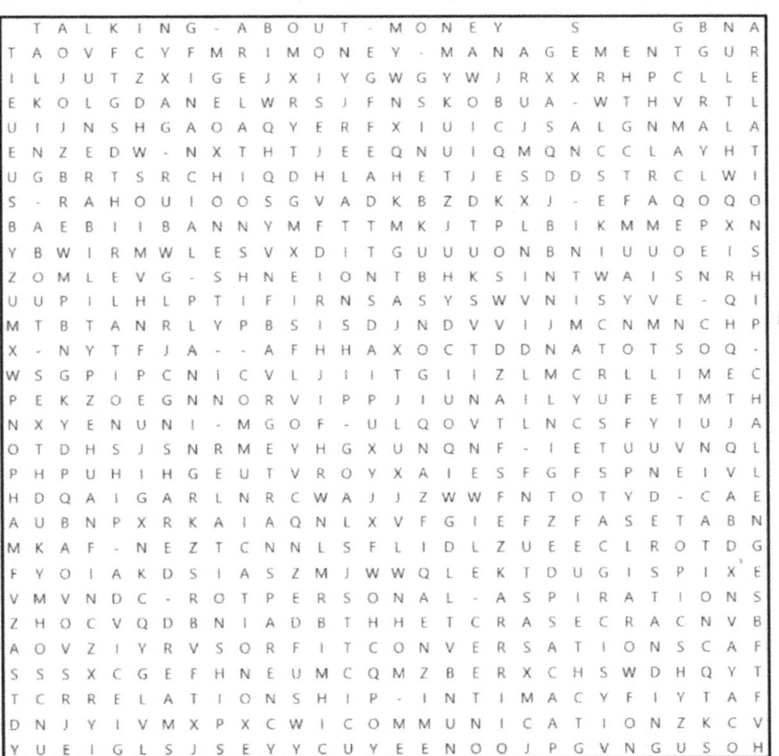

Challenges
Communication
Conversations
Difficult
Financial
Financial-planning
Honesty-in-relationships
Intimacy
Intimacy
Joint-goals

Money-management
Open-communication
Personal-aspirations
Relationship-advice
Relationship-challenges
Relationship-communication
Relationship-goals
Relationship-intimacy
Sensitive-topics

Sex-and-intimacy
Shared-dreams
Talking-about-money
Talking-about-sex
Tough-conversations
Transparency
Trust
Understanding
Vulnerability

ADDRESSING CHALLENGING TOPICS

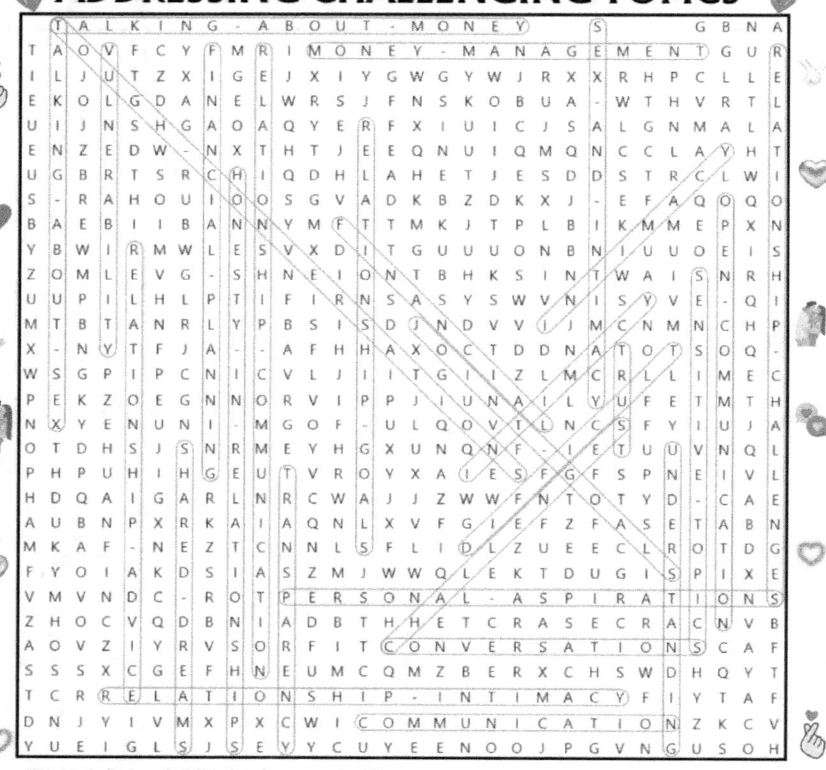

Challenges	Money-management	Sex-and-intimacy
Communication	Open-communication	Shared-dreams
Conversations	Personal-aspirations	Talking-about-money
Difficult	Relationship-advice	Talking-about-sex
Financial	Relationship-challenges	Tough-conversations
Financial-planning	Relationship-communication	Transparency
Honesty-in-relationships	Relationship-goals	Trust
Intimacy	Relationship-intimacy	Understanding
Intimacy	Sensitive-topics	Vulnerability
Joint-goals		

Chapter 5: Maintaining the Spark in Long-Term Love

Love, like a fine wine, has the potential to become richer and more complicated with time. The first spark of attraction, although exciting, is just a peek into the depths of intimacy and connection that may be developed over the course of a long-term relationship. However, as the years pass and the rhythms of everyday life set in, it is easy for that spark to wane, for the flame of passion to flicker and die. Maintaining the spark in a long-term relationship takes thought, effort, and a willingness to accept both novelty and spontaneity.

Remember the glorious early stages of your relationship, when every moment seemed like an adventure, every touch sent goosebumps down your spine, and every discussion was full of laughter and discovery. While it is impractical to expect that level of intensity to last permanently, you may replicate those sensations of excitement and passion by introducing new elements into your relationship.

Novelty is the cure to repetition. It's the exhilaration of attempting something new, moving out of your comfort zone, and sharing the satisfaction of exploring unexplored terrain together. Trying a new restaurant, going on a weekend vacation to a neighboring town, or learning a new skill together are all examples of novelty. It may even be as extravagant as going on a cross-country road trip, taking a culinary class together, or enrolling in a couples' dancing session.

The idea is to break away from the habits that have been established in your relationship and welcome the unfamiliar. Plan surprise dates, try new activities, and visit new locations together. Injecting novelty into your relationship allows for shared experiences, humor, and connection. You renew the flame of curiosity and adventure that initially brought you together.

Spontaneity is the sister of novelty, bringing a sense of surprise and unpredictability into your connection. It's the unplanned picnic in the park, the surprise love note left on the bathroom mirror, or the last-minute choice to cancel your plans and spend the day exploring a new section of town. Spontaneity interrupts the monotony of regularity and adds a feeling of fun and energy to your relationship.

While preparation is vital in many parts of life, spontaneity may be an effective strategy for maintaining romance. Never be scared to deviate from the script and embrace the unexpected. Surprise your sweetheart with a tiny present, set up an unexpected date night, or just offer a change of scenery from your typical weekend routine. Embracing spontaneity keeps your mate guessing and adds energy to your relationship.

Shared experiences are the foundation of a successful and enduring relationship. Whether it's attempting a new sport together, working for a cause you both care about, or just going for a stroll in nature, shared experiences generate lasting memories and enhance your bond. They provide possibilities for fun, connection, and personal development.

Schedule time for shared experiences in your relationship. Schedule regular date evenings, weekend trips, or even simple things such as making supper or playing a board game. Look for ways to learn and develop together, whether it's via a class, a workshop, or just reading and discussing a book.

Prioritizing shared events helps to develop a shared past, which deepens and strengthens your relationship. You accumulate a bank of pleasant memories to depend on during difficult times, and you foster a feeling of shared purpose and meaning in your relationship.

Maintaining the spark in a long-term relationship requires a willingness to go outside of your comfort zone, accept novelty and spontaneity, and emphasize shared experiences. It's about rediscovering the pleasure of adventure, the thrill of surprise, and the profound connection that comes from sharing your life with someone you care about.

Date Nights and Quality Time

In the course of a long-term relationship, the frenzy of everyday routines may easily eclipse the passion that once bloomed. Work, family, and other obligations may take up our time and energy, leaving little space for the spontaneous dates and deep discussions that previously characterized our relationship. However, prioritizing quality time together is not a luxury, but rather a need for keeping the flame of love alive.

Imagine your relationship as a garden. To bloom, love need sustenance and care, just as plants require water and sunshine. Date evenings and quality time are essential to keeping your love garden fresh and thriving. They provide a specific location for you to interact, reconnect, and rediscover the pleasure of each other's presence.

Date evenings do not need to be fancy or costly. They might be as easy as preparing supper together, watching a movie at home, or going for a stroll in the park. The trick is to schedule devoted time for just the two of you, free of distractions and commitments. Put aside your phones, switch off the television, and concentrate on one another.

On your date evenings, make an effort to actually connect with your companion. Engage in meaningful discussions, express your views and emotions, and actively listen to what others have to say. Ask open-ended inquiries, express real interest in their lives, and provide support and encouragement. Focusing on each other strengthens your emotional relationship and fosters a greater feeling of closeness.

Quality time does not necessarily need to be scheduled in advance. It might also be spontaneous and unplanned. Surprise your lover with breakfast in bed, a lunchtime love letter, or an unexpected dance party in the kitchen. Small expressions of love and devotion may go a long way toward keeping the flame alive.

Surprise and Spontaneity

There are certain times in love that shine brighter than others, moments that surprise, excite, and reignite the flame of desire. These moments are often the result of surprise and spontaneity, bringing a touch of enchantment to a relationship's daily rhythm.

Imagine arriving home to a candlelight supper, replete with your favorite dish and a handmade love message. Consider getting a surprise present because your spouse wants to demonstrate their love and gratitude, rather than for a specific occasion. These acts of spontaneity, although apparently little, may have a significant influence on the emotional landscape of your relationship.

Surprise and spontaneity disrupt the monotony of routine, bringing a feeling of fun and energy to your relationship. They remind you that love is more than simply comfort and familiarity; it's about adventure and the excitement of the unexpected. They generate shared experiences that you'll treasure for years to come, strengthening your link and increasing your closeness.

Spontaneity does not need to be spectacular or complicated. It may be as easy as surprise your spouse with a cup of coffee in bed, proposing a last-minute picnic in the park, or detouring on your way home to discover a new area. The goal is to welcome the unexpected, let go of the need for control, and let yourself get carried away by the moment.

Surprise your lover with tiny expressions of love and respect. Place a love note in their lunch bag, send them a sexy text message throughout the day, or arrange a surprise date night. These simple gestures of spontaneity inform your spouse that you are thinking about them and appreciate their presence in your life.

Break out from the norm and attempt new things together. Instead of your typical dinner and movie date, consider taking a dancing lesson, going rock climbing, or seeing a comedy performance. Explore new destinations, sample different foods, and move out of your comfort zone together. By embracing novelty, you may create shared experiences that encourage connection and leave lasting impressions.

Plan unexpected activities and retreats. Weekend trips to surrounding towns, unplanned road trips, and even staycations at local hotels may all add excitement and passion to your relationship. The element of surprise provides an added dimension of excitement, fostering a feeling of anticipation and adventure.

Puzzle Exercise

Instruction:

Find the hidden words in the puzzle. Words can be written horizontally, vertically, or diagonally, forward or backward. Circle each word you find.

At the end of your attempt, look into the completed puzzle table to find out how correct you are.

STRATEGIES FOR KEEPING THE SPARK ALIVE IN LONG-TERM RELATIONSHIPS

Adventure
Affection
Connection
Date-nights
Emotional-intimacy
Excitement
Exploration
Fun
Intimacy
Long-term-love

Novelty
Passion
Playfulness
Quality-time
Reconnection
Relationship-advice
Romance
Shared-experiences
Spontaneity
Surprise

STRATEGIES FOR KEEPING THE SPARK ALIVE IN LONG-TERM RELATIONSHIPS

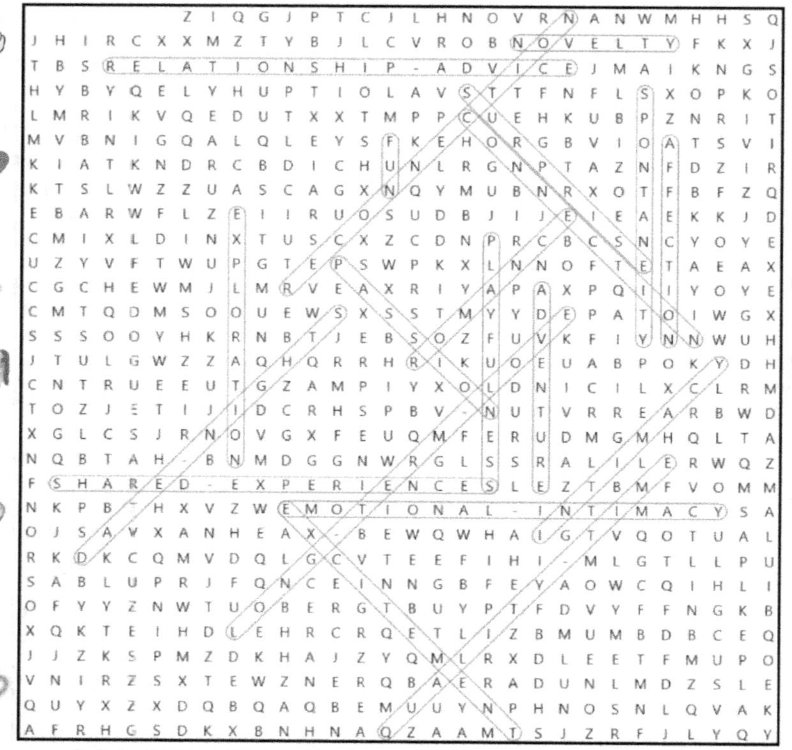

Adventure
Affection
Connection
Date-nights
Emotional-intimacy
Excitement
Exploration
Fun
Intimacy
Long-term-love

Novelty
Passion
Playfulness
Quality-time
Reconnection
Relationship-advice
Romance
Shared-experiences
Spontaneity
Surprise

Chapter 6: Overcoming Common Challenges

Even the most passionate and loving partnerships may experience turbulence. Jealousy, insecurity, and adultery are frequent obstacles that may put a relationship's strength to the test and leave lasting consequences. Nonetheless, these problems are not insurmountable. Couples that tackle these storms with open communication, understanding, forgiveness, and a determination to restore trust can emerge stronger and more bonded than ever before.

Jealousy often rears its head when we feel threatened or uncomfortable in a relationship. It might take the form of possessiveness, distrust, or even unreasonable wrath. While jealousy is normal, when it becomes excessive or baseless, it may poison a relationship and foster a poisonous environment of distrust and resentment.

Understanding the underlying reason of envy is essential for conquering it. Do you feel ignored or underappreciated by your partner? Are there unsolved trust concerns from previous relationships? Do you compare yourself to others and feel inadequate? By understanding the root reason of your jealousy, you may begin to treat it in a healthy and productive manner.

Open communication is critical. Discuss your emotions with your spouse, but avoid making accusations or assigning blame. Express your concerns calmly and rationally, concentrating on how their actions make you feel. Instead of stating, "You're always flirting with other people," try saying, "When you flirt with others, it makes me feel insecure and unimportant."

Listen to your spouse with empathy and compassion. They may not even be aware of how their actions are hurting you. By providing a secure environment for open communication, you may collaborate to create solutions that meet both of your requirements.

Insecurity, that nagging sense of self-doubt, may also harm a relationship. When we are insecure, we may doubt our partner's love, worry about being replaced, or demand continual reassurance. This may lead to a cycle of neediness and dependency, suffocating the connection.

Building self-esteem is essential for overcoming insecurity. Focus on your successes and abilities, and engage in self-care activities that benefit your mind, body, and soul. Surround yourself with supportive friends and family who will inspire and motivate you.

Communicate your anxieties to your spouse, but don't hold them accountable for your pleasure. Explain how their words and actions might intensify or relieve your anxieties. For example, instead of stating, "You never compliment me," add, "I feel more confident when you express your appreciation for me."

Remember that your spouse cannot heal your anxieties on their own. It is ultimately up to you to focus on improving your self-esteem. However, a caring and supportive spouse may play an important role in making you feel safer in yourself and your relationship.

Infidelity may destroy a relationship and leave profound emotional scars. Although the suffering may seem overwhelming, healing and forgiveness are possible. The road to recovery is long and difficult, but with open communication, honesty, and a commitment to reestablish trust, couples may emerge from this catastrophe stronger than before.

If you have been unfaithful, accept complete responsibility for your conduct. Recognize the grief you've caused your lover and show genuine regret. Be patient and empathetic as your spouse works through their feelings, and avoid getting defensive or dismissive.

If you've been deceived, allow yourself to mourn the loss of trust. Seek help from family, friends, or a therapist. Communicate your emotions to your spouse without accusing or abusing them. Focus on articulating how their actions have impacted you and what you need from them to begin healing.

Rebuilding trust requires time, effort, and consistent delivery on commitments. It requires openness, honesty, and the courage to be vulnerable. Attend couples therapy jointly, if required, to address the underlying problems that led to the infidelity and establish trust-building tactics.

Remember that forgiveness is a choice, not a duty. If you are not ready to forgive, do not push it. Take the time you need to recuperate and discuss your needs with your spouse. If you choose to forgive, do it wholeheartedly, letting go of the anger and resentment that may poison your relationship.

Overcoming issues like as jealousy, insecurity, and adultery is difficult, but it is achievable. By handling these difficulties with open communication, understanding, forgiveness, and a dedication to restore trust, you may deepen your connection and establish a more rewarding and enduring relationship.

Building Trust and Overcoming Doubts

For two persons who are in love, envy and insecurity may create lengthy shadows, hiding the warmth and pleasure that should fill the space between two hearts. These feelings, which are often interwoven, may produce distrust, anger, and a nagging sensation of discomfort, threatening to destroy the fundamental basis of a partnership.

For example, a partnership in which one half is continuously concerned about the other's faithfulness, analyzing every encounter and dissecting every gesture. Consider a situation in which one partner's anxieties about their looks or suitability for love result in a persistent desire for confirmation and affirmation. If left unchecked, these behaviors may undermine trust, create distance, and eventually lead to the breakdown of a once-loving relationship.

Understanding the source of envy and insecurity is essential for overcoming them, as is open communication and a dedication to creating trust. Jealousy is generally motivated by a fear of loss, or a perceived danger to the relationship's security. It might be triggered by prior events, personal fears, or even cultural standards.

If you're experiencing envy, consider the underlying reason. Do you feel ignored or underappreciated by your partner? Do you have unresolved trust concerns from your prior relationships? Do you compare yourself to others and feel inadequate? By identifying the source of your envy, you may begin to handle it in a healthy and helpful manner.

Discuss your emotions with your spouse, but avoid making accusations or assigning blame. Express your concerns calmly and rationally, concentrating on how their actions make you feel. Instead of stating, "You're always flirting with that coworker," try saying, "When you spend a lot of time talking to them, it makes me feel insecure."

In contrast, insecurity is typically caused by a lack of self-love and acceptance. When we don't feel good about ourselves, we may question our partner's love for us or seek continual external affirmation. Building self-esteem is an important step toward overcoming insecurity. Focus on your successes and abilities, and engage in self-care activities that benefit your mind, body, and soul. Surround yourself with good individuals who will encourage and support you.

Communicate your anxieties to your spouse, but don't hold them accountable for your pleasure. Explain how their words and actions might intensify or relieve your anxieties. For example, instead of stating, "You never compliment me," add, "I feel more confident when you express your appreciation for me."

Remember that overcoming jealousy and insecurity is a process, not a goal. It takes time, work, and courage to tackle your anxieties and weaknesses. By encouraging open communication, practicing self-love, and establishing trust, you may develop a relationship in which both parties feel comfortable, valuable, and unconditionally loved.

Healing and Rebuilding After a Breach of Trust

Infidelity may destroy trust and leave a lasting feeling of betrayal. The anguish caused by such a rupture may seem insurmountable, forcing couples to grapple with issues of forgiveness, healing, and the prospect of recreating what was lost. The path to rehabilitation is surely difficult, but it is not impossible. Couples may negotiate this challenging terrain by communicating openly, empathically, and committing to recovery together.

Acknowledging the suffering is the first step towards healing. Whether you are the one who strayed or the one who was betrayed, it is critical to understand the extent of the pain caused by infidelity. There is no way to minimize the damage or avoid the inevitable anguish, rage, and uncertainty. Allow yourself to experience these feelings and express them freely and honestly, free of judgment or shame.

Open communication is the lifeline that may lift you from the depths of sorrow. Tell your companion about your suffering, anxieties, and uncertainties. Share your future expectations and be open to hearing others'. This is not the time for blame or retribution, but rather for understanding, empathy, and a common determination to find a way ahead together.

Forgiveness is a complicated and very personal experience. It does not happen immediately, nor is it always simple. It takes a desire to let go of anger and resentment, to relinquish the grasp of the past, and to open your heart to the prospect of healing. Forgiveness does not imply endorsing the adultery or ignoring the grief it caused. It entails deciding to go ahead, to begin a new chapter in your relationship, and to accept the possibility of development and evolution.

Building trust is a lengthy and careful process. It calls for constant action, honesty, and a willingness to be vulnerable. The spouse who strayed must accept full responsibility for their actions, express real regret, and resolve to make restitution. This may include behavioral adjustments, improved transparency, and a desire to go above and beyond to restore confidence.

The betrayed partner must be willing to perform their share. This entails letting go of the need for control, abandoning the hold of mistrust, and opening their hearts to the prospect of forgiveness and reconciliation. It's crucial to remember that restoring trust requires both partners to be totally dedicated to the process.

Seeking professional assistance might be a useful resource throughout your journey. A couple's therapist can offer a secure and supportive environment in which you may examine your emotions, talk honestly, and devise ways for regaining trust. Therapy may also assist you in addressing any underlying issues that may have led to the infidelity, including as communication difficulties, unmet needs, or unresolved trauma.

Puzzle Exercise

Instruction:

Find the hidden words in the puzzle. Words can be written horizontally, vertically, or diagonally, forward or backward. Circle each word you find.

At the end of your attempt, look into the completed puzzle table to find out how correct you are.

OVERCOMING COMMON RELATIONSHIP CHALLENGES

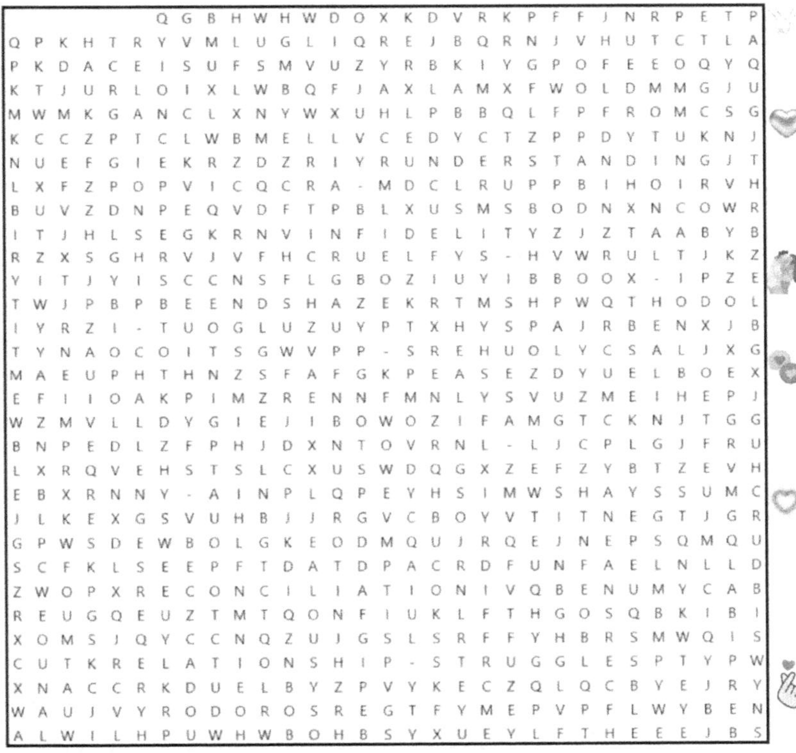

Betrayal
Communication
Couples-therapy
Emotional-healing
Forgiveness
Healing
Infidelity
Insecurity
Jealousy
Rebuilding-trust

Reconciliation
Relationship-challenges
Relationship-repair
Relationship-struggles
Self-esteem
Support
Trust-issues
Understanding
Vulnerability
Honest

OVERCOMING COMMON RELATIONSHIP CHALLENGES

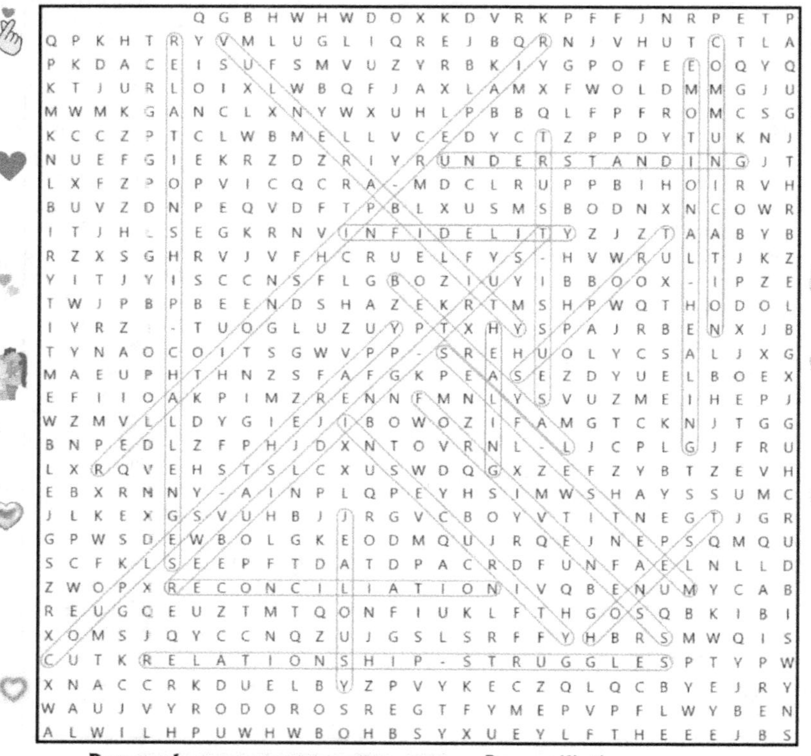

Betrayal

Communication

Couples-therapy

Emotional-healing

Forgiveness

Healing

Infidelity

Insecurity

Jealousy

Rebuilding-trust

Reconciliation

Relationship-challenges

Relationship-repair

Relationship-struggles

Self-esteem

Support

Trust-issues

Understanding

Vulnerability

Honest

Chapter 7: Communication in Different Stages of Love

Love is a dynamic journey with distinct obstacles and possibilities for development. As couples advance through these phases, their communication demands change, forcing them to adapt and develop their communication techniques in order to retain intimacy, connection, and understanding.

Communication in the early phases of a relationship, sometimes known as the honeymoon period, is usually easy and exciting. The air is heavy with excitement and expectation, and talks flow easily, motivated by a desire to understand everything about one another. This is a period of discovery in which partners express their ambitions, aspirations, and innermost wishes. Communication is often lively, flirty, and peppered with praises and affirmations.

However, once the honeymoon period ends and the reality of everyday life set in, communicating may become more difficult.

Couples may discover disparities in their personalities, values, and communication styles. Misunderstandings might occur, and disputes may increase in frequency. Couples must develop appropriate communication habits now to ensure long-term success.

Newlyweds, still basking in the afterglow of their wedding, may discover that communicating needs more work and focus. They may need to learn how to negotiate conflicts, state their wants and expectations effectively, and develop communication patterns that work for both of them. This is also an opportunity to explore common beliefs and aspirations, as well as set the framework for a future based on trust, respect, and mutual understanding.

Long-term couples who have weathered life's storms together may have unique communication issues. The initial enthusiasm and excitement may have given way to a more comfortable, regular routine. While stability may be reassuring, it can also lead to complacency and a breakdown of communication. Couples may begin to take each other for granted, believing they know what their other is thinking or feeling without having to ask.

To keep their relationship healthy and lively, long-term partners must make a concerted effort to communicate. This entails scheduling frequent time for meaningful talks, expressing appreciation and thanks, and actively listening to one another's problems and wants. It also entails being willing to adapt and progress as persons and couples, acknowledging that communication requirements may change over time.

Life changes, such as having a baby, changing employment, or dealing with loss, may all have a substantial influence on communication in a partnership. These shifts may introduce new problems, stress, and uncertainty, straining even the best connections. In these times, open and honest communication is even more important.

Couples going through life changes must establish a secure environment in which to share their worries, anxieties, and dreams for the future. They must be patient and understanding with one another, acknowledging that everyone handles change differently. It's also vital to enjoy modest victories together, as well as find ways to connect and encourage one another throughout life's ups and downs.

Effective communication is essential for every successful relationship, but it isn't always simple. It takes work, intentionality, and a willingness to adapt and evolve as your relationship develops and evolves. Understanding how communication demands change during the phases of love will provide you with the skills and methods you need to have a strong, long-lasting, and rewarding relationship with your spouse.

Newlyweds: Building a Strong Foundation for Marriage

The move from engaged to newlywed is a roller coaster of emotions, celebrations, and changes. Despite the excitement and delight, it's vital to remember that building a solid foundation for marriage takes more than simply love and good intentions. It involves open communication, mutual respect, and a desire to collaborate as a team.

Newlyweds often start marriage with a variety of expectations and dreams for the future. They may have imagined a life full with romance, adventure, and unending happiness. While these goals are absolutely feasible, it's crucial to remember that marriage involves work, compromise, and a willingness to face the inevitable problems that will come.

One of the most important components of establishing a solid foundation for marriage is developing excellent communication habits. Setting aside time for frequent check-ins allows you to freely and honestly share your thoughts, needs, and expectations. It entails carefully listening to your spouse, validating their feelings, and attempting to comprehend their viewpoint.

As newlyweds, you are still discovering one other's communication styles. You may find that one of you is more direct, whilst the other takes a softer approach. You may discover that one of you need more time alone to manage emotions, whilst the other seeks continual interaction. Understanding and appreciating these differences can help you build a communication style that works for both of you.

Creating common values and objectives is another critical component of building a solid foundation. What are your aspirations for the future? Do you want to establish a family, explore the globe, or pursue a great profession together? By openly and honestly addressing these subjects, you may develop a common vision for the future and collaborate to accomplish your objectives.

It's also critical to set limits and expectations early on. How will you manage your funds, domestic tasks, and decision making? By having these talks upfront, you may prevent future misunderstandings and animosity.

Long-Term Couples: Reconnecting and Reigniting Passion

The currents of desire in a long-term relationship may ebb and flow as time passes. The ferocious intensity of early love often fades into a soothing warmth, a deep-rooted attachment that has endured the test of time. While this progression is normal and lovely, it's crucial to remember that passion isn't a limited resource that will fade with age. It's a flame that can be lit, a spark that can be rekindled, with deliberate effort and a determination to reconnect with the heart of your loved one.

For example, a couple that has been together for decades. They have raised children, created a house, and weathered life's storms together. The everyday rituals have grown engrained, and the exhilaration of early love may seem like a distant memory. However, under the surface, a reservoir of emotion remains, ready to be tapped upon.

Reconnecting with this desire requires a willingness to view your lover through new eyes, rediscovering the traits that initially attracted you to them. Take a time to think about the early stages of your relationship. What did you appreciate most about your partner? What activities did you like doing together? What set your hearts racing and your souls singing?

By reliving these memories, you may rekindle the flame of attraction and rediscover the thrill of shared experiences. Plan a date night that recreates a great occasion from your history, visit a location with emotional importance, or just spend the evening reminiscing about the early days of your relationship.

In addition to remembering the past, it is crucial to make new memories together. Discover new hobbies or interests, travel to new places, or just check out a new restaurant in your area. The aim is to break out from the monotony of routine and provide a feeling of excitement and originality to your relationship.

Communication is also essential for reconnecting and rekindling passion. Discuss your ambitions, fantasies, and dreams with your companion. Be honest about your emotional and physical demands. Listen to your partner's point of view with empathy and compassion, and be open to compromise and collaboration to create solutions that work for both of you.

Do not be hesitant to show your love and admiration for your mate. Tell them how important they are to you, remind them of the characteristics you like, and show your thanks for their presence in your life. Small acts of kindness, such as a surprise embrace, a loving letter, or a simple "I love you," may go a long way toward reigniting the fire of romance.

Puzzle Exercise

Instruction:

Find the hidden words in the puzzle. Words can be written horizontally, vertically, or diagonally, forward or backward. Circle each word you find.

At the end of your attempt, look into the completed puzzle table to find out how correct you are.

ADAPTING COMMUNICATION STRATEGIES

```
          J G L V A B J V C W I O D Y S N V J V P Q M F J F
C O M M U N I C A T I O N - I N - M A R R I A G E H H B E F S
Z A P H H Z N O R S U K E C J X H O N E Y M O O N - P H A S E
N A S A T B V U X W W B B P S U H Q X D I O N Q E L O H S C V
G I C A I U H P J E L L R E D T L G X Y Y Y M T W G Y R A I Z
J H M L I S B L P R E C O N N E C T I O N O Y E L L B E G Y N
X M L M E L T E F E O Q J V U E I N B E Z A C U Y O Y L C S A
I L B E W I W - R Z K M P G E U M W W G D I C V W N B A O O S
B M T C F E P C V U L E A T S - J P J V V U R V E G U T T H H
R C D O U Z W O Y T X I C N K O S T L D U V T M D - J I H D N
Q U G B K T T M Y U F B O Z C C Q T A U V X M K - T V O A N Y
H A F A Y Z U M X K Z I Q X U E A - A S U O A D C E J N I E M
U J D B Y O S U W X T H M D V N P Z B G E S V Z O R Z S H R Z
M T T C C Y H N K A S R F P T I D U F W E W X B M M G H B M S
E U F T T J A I T I H K I A H X V E U X K S H V M - L I X N O
V Y B F V H R C V X X T G S F H H Y R O J J O B U R K P G W W
Z K Z M Q G E A V D Z D N S J W D N X S B M J N N E P - Q Q N
P M S L B P D T I L E O O I B E G L I J T H Q Y I L D C F D Y
C K V M X N - I P A I S H O F J X J A X U A T U C A N O Z U U
Y H M E T D E O C T X R N N K J Q J H P P V N W A T D M W U Z
X O Z J K V X N A E Y I R E E I L O Z T L Y V D T I Q M S Y N
S Q P F D Y P L R C O N N E C T I O N V X A Z K I O Y U U U S
B M E S F R E L A T I O N S H I P - S T A G E S O N M N B W B
Q B K E B R R M D G Y A G S U Q B K Z I G H M D N S G I B Z R
C O M M U N I C A T I O N - C H A N G E S G U D O H F C I G P
T D N W H T E Q W W T L E M O T I O N A L - I N T I M A C Y X
N B X K N K N U S W F T K X O B S Y G Z S S R Z D P B T M O N
S R K I L S C O M M U N I C A T I O N - S T Y L E S S I E M P
J J T D A T E - N I G H T S T M M B V J G Y V O S P W O A S G
O Y W X V G S A E V I R F K P C P X G L I F E - C H A N G E S
Y G F Y H R G P S D Z U P S Z Y X Q M L X M M H F N S B O F M
```

Communication-changes
Communication-in-marriage
Communication-styles
Connection
Couple-communication
Date-nights
Emotional-intimacy
Expectations
Honeymoon-phase
Intimacy

Life-changes
Long-term-relationships
Love-stages
Newlywed-communication
Passion
Reconnection
Relationship-advice
Relationship-communication
Relationship-stages
Romance
Shared-experiences
Understanding

ADAPTING COMMUNICATION STRATEGIES

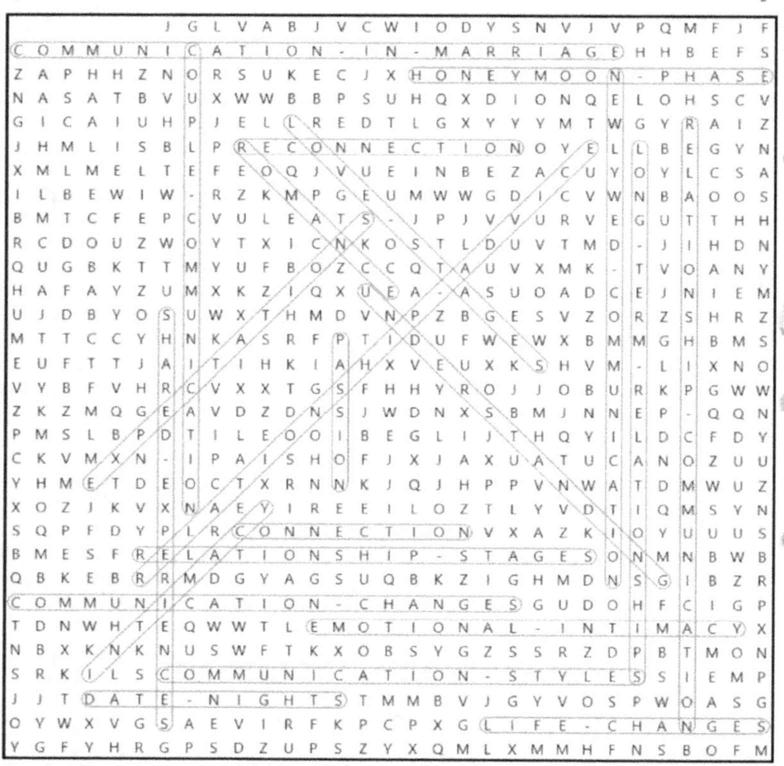

Communication-changes
Communication-in-marriage
Communication-styles
Connection
Couple-communication
Date-nights
Emotional-intimacy
Expectations
Honeymoon-phase
Intimacy

Life-changes
Long-term-relationships
Love-stages
Newlywed-communication
Passion
Reconnection
Relationship-advice
Relationship-communication
Relationship-stages
Romance
Shared-experiences
Understanding

Chapter 8: Relationship Exercises and Activities

These exercises are designed to be fun, engaging, and thought-provoking, fostering deeper connection and understanding between you and your partner. Choose one or two to try each week, and be open to exploring new ways of communicating and connecting with your loved one.

Example Entry:

Exercise: The "Highs and Lows" Check-In

Instructions:

1. Set aside dedicated time each day, perhaps during dinner or before bed, to check in with each other about your day.
2. Take turns sharing the "high" (best part) and "low" (most challenging part) of your day.
3. Listen actively and empathetically to your partner's experiences, offering support and validation.

4. Ask open-ended questions to encourage deeper conversation and understanding.

5. Reflect together on any common themes or patterns that emerge.

Benefits:

- Promotes daily connection and communication
- Encourages active listening and empathy
- Provides a safe space for sharing both positive and negative experiences
- Strengthens emotional intimacy and understanding

More Exercises and Activities:

- **"I Feel..." Statements:** Practice expressing your emotions using "I feel..." statements instead of blaming or accusing language. For example, instead of saying "You always make me angry," say "I feel frustrated when you interrupt me."

- **Weekly Relationship Meeting:** Schedule a weekly meeting to discuss any issues, concerns, or goals for your relationship. This dedicated time for communication can help prevent problems from festering and promote proactive problem-solving.

- **Appreciation Shower:** Set aside time each week to shower your partner with compliments, praise, and expressions of love and gratitude. This can be done verbally, through written notes, or through acts of service.

- **"No Phone Zone:"** Designate certain times or areas in your home as "no phone zones" where you disconnect from technology and focus solely on each other. This can be during meals, date nights, or other quality time together.

- **"Couple's Bucket List:"** Create a list of shared experiences, adventures, and goals you want to achieve together. This can be a fun and inspiring way to plan your future and create lasting memories.

- **"Listening Without Fixing:"** Practice listening to your partner without offering advice or solutions. Sometimes, all your partner needs is a compassionate ear and a safe space to vent his/her feelings.

- **"Compliment Challenge:"** Each day, challenge yourselves to give each other three genuine compliments. Focus on specific qualities, actions, or traits that you admire in each other.

- **"Shared Journal:"** Keep a shared journal where you can write love notes, share your thoughts and feelings, or simply document your daily experiences together. This can be a beautiful way to connect and create a lasting record of your love story.

Conclusion

As we near the conclusion of our voyage across the terrain of love and communication, it is evident that the way to a long-term and successful relationship requires purpose, effort, and a thorough knowledge of both ourselves and our partners. It's a journey that demands us to be vulnerable, talk frankly and honestly, and develop understanding, compassion, and forgiveness.

The techniques and tactics discussed in this book are neither magic formula or fast cures. They serve as guideposts, providing guidance and support as you negotiate the complexity of love and relationships. They are invitations to deepen your connection, strengthen your relationship, and cultivate a love that will last the test of time.

Remember that good communication is more than simply the words we say; it's also about how we listen, touch, and demonstrate our love and admiration. It is about knowing our partner's needs, appreciating their differences, and finding common ground even when there are disputes.

It's about accepting vulnerability, expressing our worries and vulnerabilities, and enabling our partner to fully see and understand us. It's about celebrating one other's accomplishments, encouraging one another's aspirations, and developing a common vision for the future.

Most significantly, it emphasizes never giving up on love. Relationships are not always easy, but they are always worth fighting for. You may establish a love that is not only long-lasting but also genuinely rewarding by devoting time, energy, and effort to communicating.

So, talk it out. Express your wants, objectives, and concerns clearly and honestly. Listen to your spouse with empathy and compassion. Seek out compromises, work together to find solutions, and appreciate your differences.

Walk it through. Turn your words into action. Show your love by doing acts of service, making meaningful gestures, and spending quality time together. Embrace physical contact, try new things, and make lasting memories.

Make it last. Nurture your love with focus and care. Prioritize your relationship, work on your communication skills, and never stop learning and developing together. Remember that love is a journey, not a destination. By accepting the trials and appreciating the victories along the road, you may cultivate a love that not only lasts a lifetime but also improves every minute of your lives.

Remember that you are not alone on this path. Countless couples have traveled this route before you, confronting similar struggles and successes. Seek advice from reliable friends, family members, or experts as required. Read books, take seminars, and look into resources to assist you improve your knowledge of love and communication.

Most essential, trust in the strength of love. Believe that you and your spouse are capable of overcoming any hurdle, healing any pain, and creating an exceptional love.

BOOK 2: UNLEASHING HEALTHY RELATIONSHIPS

Techniques to Restore Love and Build Lasting Connection

Introduction

In our everyday life, we desire for deep, meaningful relationships. We are in constant search for that particular person who understands us, encourages us, and shares our happiness and sorrows. We seek the warmth of closeness, the comfort of company, and the assurance that we are loved unconditionally.

But what exactly does it mean to have a healthy relationship? It's not only about finding the perfect person; it's about nurturing a relationship that flourishes, matures, and stands the test of time. A healthy relationship is a bright bond made from trust, respect, communication, and constant support. It's a safe place where both partners feel safe to be themselves, without fear of criticism or rejection.

Healthy relationships are not only necessary for our emotional well-being, but they also play an important role in our general health and happiness. According to studies, people in meaningful relationships have lower levels of stress, better mental health, and even a stronger immune system. When we feel loved and connected, we are more resilient to life's obstacles, more inspired to achieve our objectives, and more likely to have a strong sense of purpose and satisfaction.

However, developing and sustaining a good relationship takes work, dedication, and a desire to learn and develop together. A relationship, like a plant, requires ongoing care and attention to thrive. It's about realizing that love is a journey, a never-ending process of discovery, understanding, and deeper connection.

This book is your road map to realizing the full potential of your relationship. It is a handbook for individuals who want to create a love that lasts, empowers, and changes. Whether you're just starting out in a relationship or have been together for years, the ideas and practices provided in these pages will give you the skills you need to form an unbreakable connection.

We will dig into the underlying concepts that drive good relationships, such as the power of communication, the value of trust, and the art of dispute resolution. You'll discover how to rekindle desire, cultivate intimacy, and build shared purpose with your spouse. We will also discuss the inevitable obstacles that emerge in every relationship, including advice on forgiving, healing, and moving ahead together.

This book includes practical activities, thought-provoking questions, to help you apply these ideas to your own unique relationship. We hope that by accepting the knowledge presented in these pages, you can not only enhance your current tie, but also uncover new levels of love, connection, and pleasure.

So, if you're ready to go on a revolutionary journey to unlock the potential of healthy relationships, let's start. Together, we will discover the route to long-term love, satisfaction, and an endlessly exciting future.

Chapter 1: Understanding the Foundations of Healthy Relationships

Before embarking on the path to this healthy journey, we must first have a clear grasp of the basic building blocks that constitute the basis of a successful relationship. These fundamental qualities serve as the pillars around which love, trust, and connection are created, offering a stable foundation for navigating life's inevitable obstacles and rewards.

A good relationship is based on mutual respect. This includes appreciating your partner's views, emotions, and opinions, even if they vary from your own. It entails treating people with respect, care, and civility, both privately and publicly. Respect also entails acknowledging and appreciating your partner's limits, promoting their uniqueness, and never engaging in insulting or degrading actions.

Open and honest communication is another essential component of a good relationship. It entails communicating your opinions, emotions, and wants in a straightforward and direct way while actively listening to your partner's viewpoint. Effective communication promotes understanding, trust, and avoids misunderstandings from escalating into bigger confrontations. It is the lifeblood that keeps the connection alive and growing.

Trust is the foundation of a successful and long-lasting connection. It entails confidence in your partner's integrity, honesty, and dependability. It entails feeling safe in their love and dedication, knowing that they have your back and will support you through thick and thin. Trust is not blind faith; it is gained by consistent behavior, honest communication, and a willingness to be vulnerable with one another.

Emotional support is an important aspect of a good relationship. It entails being there for your partner in both good and terrible times, lending a listening ear, a shoulder to weep on, or a word of encouragement. Emotional support is empathizing with your partner's emotions, acknowledging their experiences, and offering comfort and reassurance as required. It is about providing a secure environment in which both partners may feel loved, understood, and supported.

Shared ideals and objectives are also necessary for a successful collaboration. While you don't have to agree on everything, having a broad agreement on essential life values like family, profession, and personal improvement may help you feel connected and purposeful. Shared objectives, such as travel, property, or establishing a family, may create a feeling of purpose and enthusiasm for the future.

Physical closeness is an integral part of many love partnerships. It's a method to show love, affection, and desire. However, it is crucial to realize that physical closeness is not limited to sex. It also involves snuggling, kissing, holding hands, and other types of physical contact. The amount of physical intimacy in a relationship will differ from couple to couple, but it is critical that both parties be comfortable and content with the level of physical contact.

In addition to these beneficial patterns, there are several typical harmful habits that may negate the basis of a relationship and lead to conflict. This may include:

- Poor communication between spouses may lead to misunderstandings, animosity, and weakened bonds.
- Belittling, insulting, or disparaging your spouse may create a toxic atmosphere and lower their self-esteem.

- Broken trust may be difficult to repair. Suspicion, envy, and insecurity may taint a relationship, making it impossible to progress.

- Controlling or manipulating your partner's behavior, thoughts, or emotions is considered emotional abuse and may be detrimental to the relationship.

- Codependency: Relying on a spouse for happiness and self-worth may lead to an unhealthy dynamic and hinder both partners' independent growth.

Understanding the basic aspects that make a good relationship, as well as identifying the warning signals of unhealthy behaviors, allows you to take proactive efforts toward developing and maintaining a strong, meaningful, and long-lasting connection.

Defining Healthy Relationships

Healthy relationships are not based on fairy tales or ephemeral moments of passion. They are based on a thorough grasp and respect of what genuinely makes a relationship work. While each relationship is unique, there are some characteristics that distinguish those that last.

A healthy relationship is one in which both parties feel free to be themselves without fear of being judged or rejected. It's a place where people accept their weaknesses and appreciate their uniqueness. In this supportive atmosphere, both people and couples may mature and develop.

A good relationship is based on mutual respect. This includes appreciating one other's views, emotions, and opinions, even if they vary. It entails paying attention, speaking politely, and treating one another with respect and civility. Respect goes beyond words and deeds to reflect a genuine understanding for your partner's inherent value and dignity.

Trust is another essential component of a strong partnership. It is the notion that your spouse is trustworthy, honest, and has your best interests in mind. Trust is not given easily; it is earned by consistent behavior, honest communication, and a willingness to be vulnerable. When trust is there, it fosters a feeling of security, allowing both parties to feel comfortable taking chances and being themselves.

Open and honest communication is essential in every good relationship. It entails communicating your opinions, emotions, and wants in a straightforward and direct way while actively listening to your partner's viewpoint. Effective communication promotes understanding, trust, and prevents misunderstandings from turning into bigger confrontations. It's an ongoing process of sharing, listening, and reacting with understanding and compassion.

Emotional support is another critical component of a strong partnership. It entails being there for your partner through thick and thin, lending a listening ear, a shoulder to weep on, or a word of encouragement. It entails empathizing with their emotions, acknowledging their experiences, and offering comfort and reassurance as required. Emotional support offers a secure atmosphere in which both partners may feel loved, understood, and valued.

Healthy partnerships need a mix of uniqueness and connection. While spending quality time together and cultivating similar interests is crucial, it is also critical to preserve one's own identity and pursue unique hobbies and ambitions. A healthy relationship enables both parties to develop and thrive, both individually and as a pair.

Healthy relationships are not flawless; they will always have obstacles and arguments. However, the key is to approach these issues with a desire to collaborate, solve problems, and learn from the process. It is about accepting conflict as a normal component of every relationship and utilizing it to foster development and greater understanding.

Identifying Unhealthy Patterns

While knowing the wonderful features of a healthy relationship is critical, it is also necessary to shed a light on the shadows—the destructive behaviors that may quietly destroy the foundation we've created. Recognizing these behaviors is the first step toward correcting them and avoiding them from inflicting long-term harm.

One of the most prevalent harmful practices is a lack of communication. When partners retreat, get defensive, or turn to criticism and blame, the channels of communication strain. Unresolved disagreements may linger under the surface, causing anger and alienation.

Another warning indicator is a lack of trust. This may be shown as dishonesty, infidelity, or a violation of trust. When trust is broken, it leaves a profound hurt that is tough to repair. It makes both parties feel vulnerable and insecure, throwing doubt on the whole partnership.

Control and manipulation are also poisonous factors that may destabilize a connection. Attempts to control, isolate, or compel your partner are not acceptable. This conduct may take subtle forms, such as guilt-tripping, gaslighting, or withholding love. Over time, it might lower your partner's self-esteem and create a power imbalance.

Disrespect is another negative element that may destabilize a partnership. It may take various forms, including name-calling and put-downs, as well as disregarding or discounting your partner's emotions and thoughts. Disrespect undermines the basis of love, creating an atmosphere of hatred and resentment.

Codependency, which is sometimes disguised as love and loyalty, may be as harmful. When one spouse becomes unduly dependent on the other for happiness and self-esteem, it may limit personal development and create an unhealthy dynamic. Both partners must keep their own identities and pursue their own interests outside of the partnership.

Recognizing these harmful tendencies does not involve assigning blame or condemning your spouse. It's about recognizing the forces that might erode love and attachment. By understanding these habits, you may begin to address them and create a better, more meaningful relationship. Remember that even the strongest relationships may experience difficulties, but with awareness, communication, and a determination to develop, you can overcome any hurdle and maximize the potential of your love.

Chapter 2: Communication: The Heartbeat of Connection

Communication is the lifeblood of relationships, nourishing the bond between two people. It is the link that enables us to express our ideas, emotions, and desires, promoting connection, comprehension, and a strong sense of belonging. Even the most ardent love may wither and die in the absence of adequate communication, leaving an emptiness of unsaid words and unfulfilled needs.

At its core, communication is more than simply exchanging information; it is the skill of actually connecting with another individual. It entails not just stating our truth, but also carefully listening to the unsaid signals communicated by tone of voice, body language, and facial expressions. It takes understanding, compassion, and a desire to view the world through our partner's eyes.

When communication is free and real, it offers a secure environment for vulnerability, intimacy, and emotional connection. We feel heard, seen, and understood, which deepens our link and enables us to face life's obstacles together. On the other side, when communication fails, misunderstandings emerge, animosity grows, and the relationship's basis crumbles.

Active listening is one of the most effective ways to improve communication skills. This is giving your whole attention to your partner, concentrating on their words, and reflecting back what you hear to assure comprehension. It entails putting away distractions, preconceptions, and preconceived assumptions in order to really understand their point of view.

Another important part of successful communication is the ability to properly express emotions. Many of us struggle to express our emotions, particularly when they are complicated or difficult. However, concealing emotions may lead to anger, misunderstandings, and a loss of connection with our spouse. Learning to recognize and communicate our emotions in a healthy manner is critical for developing closeness and trust.

Navigating uncomfortable talks is a necessary aspect of every partnership. Conversations about economics, parental issues, or personal difficulties may be laden with tension and anxiety. However, neglecting them may lead to lingering bitterness and a developing schism between spouses. Approaching tough talks with honesty, respect, and a desire to establish common ground may result in increased understanding, intimacy, and a closer relationship.

Couples may enhance their communication skills via a variety of practical strategies and approaches. Examples include setting up regular time for undisturbed communication, practicing active listening, utilizing "I" expressions to communicate sentiments, and avoiding blame and criticism. Couples therapy or communication seminars may also be beneficial for developing new skills and strengthening relationships.

It's crucial to remember that communication is two-way. Both parties must be willing to make an effort to listen, express themselves, and work through issues together. Misunderstandings will arise from time to time, which is OK. What important is a desire to learn from those experiences, apologize if needed, and continue to develop as a pair.

The benefits of promoting good communication are tremendous. It may increase closeness, build trust, and foster a feeling of safety and security in the relationship. It may also result in increased contentment, happiness, and fulfillment for both couples. So, let us embrace the power of communication and utilize it to maximize the potential of our relationships. Let us share our truths with love, listen with compassion, and build a relationship that goes beyond words.

Mastering Effective Communication

To completely realize the potential of your relationship, you must begin on a journey to learn the skill of effective communication. This is more than just sharing words; it requires a thorough grasp of how to connect with your partner on a deep level, both vocally and nonverbally.

Begin by creating an atmosphere of openness and trust in which both partners feel comfortable expressing their views, emotions, and desires without fear of being judged or criticized. Create an environment in which vulnerability is encouraged and honesty is prized above all else.

Active listening involves actively engaging with your partner's words and feelings. Pay attention to both what they say and how they say it. Observe their tone of speech, body language, and facial expressions. Reflect on what you've heard to verify comprehension and demonstrate that you're actually there.

Be aware of your own communication style. Speak with love and respect, utilizing "I" phrases to describe your emotions and wants. Do not blame, criticize, or insult your spouse. Instead, concentrate on creating solutions and collaborating as a team.

Recognize that communication is more than simply words. Nonverbal signals like touch, eye contact, and physical closeness may send strong expressions of affection, support, and connection. Be attentive of your body language and attempt to create a welcoming environment for your partner.

Accept uncomfortable talks as chances for development and better understanding. Avoid brushing problems under the rug or assuming they will miraculously vanish. Instead, confront them front on with understanding, compassion, and a desire to establish common ground.

Active Listening: The Key to Understanding

Active listening is a powerful communication strategy that may unlock deeper understanding, promote empathy, and enhance the links of connection within a relationship. It's more than just hearing what your spouse says; it's about being totally present, engaged, and responsive to the signals sent by their tone, body language, and emotions.

Active listening is a purposeful decision to concentrate your attention on your partner and their experience. It entails putting away distractions, preconceptions, and assumptions in order to fully hear what they have to offer. It entails listening with your ears, heart, and intellect.

When you practice active listening, you provide your partner a secure place to express oneself genuinely. You affirm their sentiments, respect their point of view, and show a real interest in what they have to say. This, in turn, increases the level of trust and closeness in the relationship.

Active listening is more than just keeping quiet while your companion talks. It needs you to interact with them, both vocally and nonverbally. This might involve nodding your head to indicate comprehension, keeping eye contact, asking clarifying questions, and summarizing what you've heard for accuracy.

By reflecting back your partner's words and sentiments, you show that you are not just listening but also comprehending the underlying emotions and meanings of their message. This confirmation may be quite powerful, creating a feeling of intimacy and connection that transcends words.

Active listening isn't always simple. It takes patience, empathy, and the ability to momentarily set aside your own ideas and emotions. However, the advantages are tremendous. When you actually listen to your spouse, you foster deeper understanding, more closeness, and a more rewarding connection.

So, the next time your spouse wants to chat, put down your phone, switch off the television, and give them your whole attention. Pay attention to what they say, what they do with their bodies, and how they feel. Reflect on what you've heard, ask clarifying questions, and verify their experience. Active listening may help you achieve a new level of connection and intimacy in your relationship, strengthening your bond and fostering long-lasting love.

Chapter 3: Reigniting Passion and Intimacy

There are seasons of flaming desire and seasons of comforting familiarity on the romantic journey. While these are crucial components of a long-term relationship, it is not unusual for the early spark to fade over time. The demands of everyday life, the buildup of stress, and the gradual loss of novelty may all lead to a decrease in desire and closeness.

But don't worry; the spark that once blazed brilliantly may be reignited. Rekindling the spark in your relationship is not only achievable, but also necessary for sustaining a strong and meaningful bond. It takes a desire to venture beyond of your comfort zone, to prioritize your partner, and to devote time and energy to cultivating the emotional and physical closeness that connects you together.

Creating possibilities for romance is an important first step. It's about enriching your relationship with simple but meaningful acts that remind your spouse of your love and admiration. It may be a surprise date night, a sincere love letter slipped into their lunchbox, or a simple act of kindness, such as preparing their favorite breakfast. The trick is to make your spouse feel unique, valued, and loved.

Spontaneity is another effective instrument for reigniting desire. Break away from the monotony of routine and add some spice to your relationship. Plan a weekend away, try a new activity together, or just surprise your lover with an unexpected kiss or embrace. Accept the unexpected and allow yourself to be fun and adventurous.

Shared experiences are the glue that holds couples together. They leave a lasting impression, build connection, and offer a feeling of shared purpose. Make time for hobbies that both of you like, such as hiking, cooking, dancing, or just snuggling together on the sofa and watching a movie. Engaging in things that offer you delight strengthens your link and fosters a stronger feeling of connection.

Emotional closeness is as vital as physical intimacy. It entails establishing a safe environment for vulnerability, in which both partners feel free to share their ideas, emotions, and anxieties without being judged. It entails actively listening to one other, validating one another's experiences, and providing support and encouragement. Emotional connection is the foundation of a healthy and long-lasting relationship.

Of course, physical contact is essential for rekindling romance. It's more than simply sex; it's about expressing love, passion, and desire via physical contact. It might be as easy as holding hands, snuggling on the sofa, or exchanging passionate kisses. Physical intimacy causes the production of oxytocin, known as the "love hormone," which enhances the link between lovers and fosters emotions of closeness and trust.

To rekindle your relationship, spending quality time together. In the hustle and bustle of everyday life, it's tempting to put your relationship on the back burner. However, spending time for each other, even if just for a few minutes each day, may make a huge impact. Put aside your phones, disengage from technology, and just be present with one another.

Communication is also essential for rekindling desire and closeness. Openly and honestly express your wishes, needs, and dreams. Share your admiration for one another, show your love and thanks, and don't be hesitant to make physical touch. Communicating freely and honestly fosters a greater sense of closeness and connection.

Creating Opportunities for Romance

In the desire to revive love and connection, understanding the art of generating romantic possibilities is a valuable ability. It's about incorporating moments of enchantment into your daily life, surprise your spouse with unexpected acts of love, and reminding them of your unique bond.

Romance does not need to be grandiose or costly. Small, thoughtful deeds typically make the most impact. A handwritten love note left on the bathroom mirror, a surprise picnic in the park, or a simple bouquet of their favorite flowers may all communicate volumes and make your spouse feel valued and treasured.

Consider your partner's love language and make romantic gestures appropriately. If they cherish acts of service, surprise them by doing a duty they loathe or cooking a special dinner. If they value words of affirmation, send them a meaningful note or whisper sweet nothings into their ear. Understanding and meeting their specific demands and preferences can make your romantic efforts much more meaningful.

Don't underestimate the value of physical contact. A warm hug, delicate caress, or long kiss may create desire and strengthen your bond. Make time for sofa cuddling, hand-holding while strolling, or a simple back massage after a hard day. Small gestures of physical love may convey a lot of information and foster feelings of connection and closeness.

Date evenings are a traditional method to spark passion. They provide a concentrated time for you and your spouse to reconnect, free of the distractions of everyday life. Date evenings, whether it's a candlelight meal at home, a movie night beneath the stars, or a romantic walk through a moonlight park, allow couples to reconnect and renew their romance.

Remember that romance is more than simply great gestures; it is about enriching your daily life with love and gratitude. Place a beautiful note in their lunchbox, send them a sexy text message throughout the day, or surprise them with their favorite coffee on their way to work. Small acts of kindness may help keep the flame alive.

Nurturing Emotional and Physical Intimacy

Beyond romantic gestures and shared experiences, a really satisfying relationship is built on a deeper level of connection: emotional and physical intimacy. These two connected components of love nurture the spirit and awaken the senses, resulting in a relationship that goes beyond the ordinary.

Emotional connection is the foundation of a sustainable relationship. It is the experience of being deeply seen, heard, and understood by your spouse. It is about expressing your innermost fears, hopes, and weaknesses without fear of being judged or rejected. It's about providing a secure environment in which you can both reveal your genuine self while feeling unconditionally loved and welcomed.

Emotional closeness needs open and honest conversation, attentive listening, and a willingness to be vulnerable. It's about communicating your ideas and emotions, even the unpleasant ones, and being open to your partner's experiences. It is about demonstrating understanding and compassion, even when disputes happen.

Physical intimacy, on the other hand, is a language of love expressed via touch, tenderness, and physical connection. It's the comfort of a hug, the tenderness of a kiss, and the intensity of a shared embrace. Physical intimacy is more than just sex; it includes a variety of manifestations, from holding hands and snuggling to playful touches and sensuous caresses.

Physical closeness is nurtured by providing chances for contact and love. It's about finding time to cuddle on the sofa, go for a stroll together, or just provide a consoling touch when your spouse is down. It's about exploring each other's bodies and wants, as well as discovering new methods to convey love and affection via physical contact.

Emotional and physical connection are required for a healthy and satisfying relationship. They complement and reinforce one another, fostering a stronger feeling of connection and intimacy. When both are there, the connection flourishes and the flame of love becomes brighter.

Nurturing closeness requires time, effort, and a willingness to be vulnerable. It takes both parties to be present, involved, and willing to try new methods of connecting. However, the advantages are tremendous. A relationship with strong emotional and physical intimacy is a source of pleasure, comfort, and constant support, as well as a safe place for both partners to grow.

Chapter 4: Turning Challenges into Growth

In the tapestry of love, conflict is an unavoidable thread that runs through the very fabric of our closest relationships. It's the natural result of two people with different ideas, beliefs, and needs joining together to create a life. While confrontation may be unpleasant and even painful, it does not have to be harmful. In reality, when tackled with the proper mentality and techniques, disagreement can serve as a catalyst for development, understanding, and deeper connection.

Recognizing that conflict is unavoidable is the first step in navigating it. No relationship is immune to conflicts, misunderstandings, and differences of opinion. Attempting to avoid confrontation is not only unachievable, but also damaging to the relationship's health. Suppressed frustrations may fester and worsen, ultimately bursting in disastrous ways.

Instead of avoiding confrontation, we might learn to see it as a chance for development and greater understanding. By changing our viewpoint, we may see disagreement as an opportunity to learn more about ourselves, our spouse, and the dynamics of our relationship. It may help us discover places where we need to enhance communication, compromise, or just demonstrate greater compassion and understanding.

Identifying the fundamental cause of conflict is critical to developing successful solutions. What seems to be a simple dispute on the surface may really be the result of deeper, underlying concerns. It might be a disagreement in ideals, unmet needs, unresolved previous wounds, or just a breakdown in communication. Taking the effort to investigate the fundamental cause may help us address the problem at its source, rather than merely addressing the symptoms.

Open and honest communication is an excellent technique to identify the fundamental cause of conflict. This entails providing a secure environment in which both partners feel free to communicate their ideas, emotions, and needs without fear of judgment or condemnation. It also requires active listening, in which we actually hear and comprehend our partner's point of view, even if we disagree with it.

Once the underlying problem has been discovered, we may start developing healthy conflict resolution solutions. This entails finding solutions that benefit both parties, rather than one winning at the cost of the other. Compromise is essential, as is the courage to let go of the need to be right all the time.

Successful dispute resolution requires effective communication abilities. This involves utilizing "I" expressions to communicate sentiments, avoiding blaming and accusations, and concentrating on the current problem rather than revisiting previous complaints. It also entails being aware of our tone of voice and body language, which may express as much meaning as our words.

Seeking help from a therapist or counselor may also be therapeutic, particularly if fighting has become an ongoing or damaging habit in the relationship. A neutral third person may provide assistance, improve communication, and assist couples in developing new healthy conflict resolution skills.

Understanding the Roots of Conflict

To properly handle conflict and turn it into an opportunity for progress, we must first investigate its causes. Like a detective looking for clues, we must go underneath the surface of our arguments to identify the underlying causes that are fueling them.

Often, what starts a disagreement is only a symptom of larger, unresolved issues. It might be an apparently little disagreement over domestic tasks that conceals a sense of being undervalued or neglected. It might be a heated financial dispute that displays competing values and interests. Alternatively, it might be a reoccurring conflict regarding parenting approaches caused by unresolved childhood traumas.

Recognizing that disagreement is seldom about the subject at hand allows us to begin to investigate the root reasons. This necessitates a willingness to stand back from the current circumstance and consider the larger context of our connection. To address conflict, it's important to consider unfulfilled needs and aspirations.

- Have any old injuries or resentments not been adequately addressed?
- Is communication successful, or are there misunderstandings?
- Are external pressures, such job or family concerns, contributing to the tension?

Understanding the underlying reasons of conflict requires open and honest dialogue. It entails establishing a secure environment in which both partners feel free to communicate their ideas, emotions, and needs without fear of judgment or condemnation. It entails actively listening to one another, attempting to comprehend the other's point of view, and being open to compromise.

It might be difficult to identify the core reasons of conflict. It may include delving deeply into our own prior experiences, investigating our own values and views, and being open about our own flaws. However, the results are definitely worth the effort.

Understanding the main causes of conflict allows us to go beyond surface-level arguments and address the underlying problems that drive the conflict. This enables us to identify solutions that are more likely to be sustainable and enjoyable for both parties. It also helps us develop as individuals and as a couple, improving our knowledge of one another and strengthening our bonds.

Healthy Conflict Resolution Strategies

When conflicts eventually emerge, as they do in all relationships, the way to resolution does not include avoidance or anger, but rather the adoption of constructive tactics that promote understanding and progress. These tactics serve as a compass, leading couples through the turbulent seas of dispute and into the calmer waters of compromise and connection.

First and first, handling conflict in a calm and transparent manner is critical. Instead of responding quickly or defensively, take a deep breath and allow yourself to genuinely understand your partner's point of view. Remember that the aim is not to win the disagreement, but to find a solution that addresses both of your wants and emotions.

Active listening is essential for effective dispute resolution. It entails not just listening to your partner's words, but also observing their tone of voice, body language, and underlying feelings. By attentively listening, you show respect, acknowledge their sentiments, and establish a secure environment for free discussion.

Expressing your own feelings and demands in a transparent and courteous manner is equally vital. Instead of criticizing or condemning your spouse, consider how their behavior or words affect you. Use "I" sentences to explain your point of view, such as "I feel hurt when..." or "I need you to..."

Finding common ground is often the key to settling conflicts. This entails establishing common principles, aims, or interests that may serve as the basis for compromise. It may also need adaptability and a readiness to let go of the urge to be correct all the time.

Brainstorming ideas together might be an effective method to go ahead. Encourage your spouse to discuss their thoughts and be willing to consider other choices. Remember that there is no one-size-fits-all answer, and the optimum strategy may include a variety of tactics.

Taking a break from the talk might be beneficial, particularly when emotions are running high. It helps both parties to calm down, think on the situation, and rejoin the talk with a clearer mind. However, it is critical to schedule a follow-up meeting to address the problem rather than ignoring it.

If you find yourself trying to handle disagreement on your own, don't be afraid to seek outside assistance. Couples therapy or counseling may offer a secure environment for communication, advice on healthy conflict resolution tactics, and assistance in managing complicated challenges.

Chapter 5: Building Trust: The Bedrock of Lasting Love

In the broad landscape of love, trust stands as a steadfast pillar, sustaining the fundamental foundation upon which strong and enduring partnerships are constructed. It is the invisible glue that holds two souls together, creating a feeling of safety, vulnerability, and profound connection. Without trust, love falters, closeness dwindles, and the possibility for development and pleasure is limited.

Trust is more than just believing that your spouse will not harm you; it is a deep feeling of trust in their character, integrity, and unshakable commitment. It's knowing that they have your back, that they will stick with you through thick and thin, and that they will always act in your best interests.

Building trust requires time, effort, and consistent action. It cannot be demanded or coerced; it must be earned via a succession of modest, daily exchanges that indicate dependability, honesty, and respect. It is about showing up when you say you will, keeping your promises, and carrying out your obligations.

Open and honest communication is a critical aspect in creating trust. This is communicating your ideas, emotions, and needs to your spouse in a straightforward and direct way, without fear of judgment or criticism. It also entails carefully listening to your partner's viewpoint, acknowledging their experiences, and displaying empathy and understanding.

Consistency is another important aspect of trust. When your actions match your words, it gives a feeling of predictability and dependability, which promotes trust. This entails being constant in your conduct, communication, and treatment of your relationship. It entails continuously showing up for them, both emotionally and physically, and being someone they can rely on.

Respect is also vital for establishing trust. This includes appreciating your partner's views, emotions, and opinions, even if they vary from your own. It entails treating people with respect, care, and civility, both privately and publicly. Respect also entails recognizing your partner's limits, valuing their uniqueness, and never engaging in insulting or degrading actions.

Transparency is another critical component of trust. This entails being upfront and honest about your ideas, emotions, and behaviors. It entails not concealing information from your relationship or holding secrets. When you are transparent, you generate a feeling of openness and honesty that develops trust and strengthens your relationship.

Trust demands consistent work and care. It's about consistently expressing your dedication to the relationship, putting your partner's well-being first, and making decisions that build your connection. It's about being aware of your behaviors and words, and always working to be the best partner you can be.

When trust is shattered, it may be disastrous for a relationship. However, this is not always the end. Rebuilding trust is achievable, but it needs both parties to admit the pain, accept responsibility for their acts, and commit to the healing process.

The first step in reestablishing trust is to recognize the anguish and hurt created by the betrayal. This requires open and honest conversation in which both parties communicate their emotions and desires. It also requires a heartfelt apology from the individual who violated the trust, acknowledging full responsibility for their conduct and expressing regret.

The next stage is to reestablish trust with regular action. This entails building trust over time by consistent conduct, open communication, and a renewed commitment to the partnership. It also entails making apologies for previous harm, whether via words, acts, or both.

The Importance of Trust in Relationships

In the complicated web of human connection, trust emerges as the foundation upon which love and intimacy thrive. It's an unconscious pact between two spirits, a subtle pledge that says, "You are secure with me. "I will cherish and protect your heart." Trust is the basis on which we may construct our ambitions, aspirations, and futures together.

Without trust, a relationship is like a building constructed on shifting sand, susceptible to even the smallest earthquake. It fosters an atmosphere of ambiguity, distrust, and dread in which love cannot flourish. When trust is gone, we continuously question our partner's motivations, mistrust their statements, and are hesitant to divulge our most intimate weaknesses.

However, when trust exists, it provides a safe and secure environment in which both partners may be their real selves. It enables us to let our guard down, be vulnerable, and express our actual emotions without fear of being judged or rejected. It gives us the courage to pursue new levels of intimacy, take chances, and evolve as a pair.

Trust is more than just thinking that our spouse will not harm us; it is also understanding that they have our best interests in mind. It's about being confident in their love and devotion, knowing that they'll be there for us through thick and thin. It's about believing in their honesty, integrity, and dependability.

When trust exists, it pervades all aspects of the relationship. It enables us to talk freely and honestly, settle disagreements constructively, and encourage one another's hopes and objectives. It fosters a sense of togetherness and collaboration, with both partners feeling appreciated, respected, and powerful.

Trust is not something that comes easily; it must be earned by constant action, honest communication, and a willingness to be vulnerable. It's an ongoing process of showing up for one another, maintaining pledges, and following through on commitments. It's about being dependable and trustworthy, and always working to be the greatest partner you can be.

When trust is destroyed, it may seem like the end of the world. However, it is vital to realize that even the greatest partnerships may face difficulties. Trust may be regained by honest conversation, forgiveness, and a commitment to rebuilding. It may require time, effort, and patience, but the benefits are tremendous. A trusting partnership may weather life's storms and emerge stronger than before.

Rebuilding Trust After Betrayal

Betrayal may destroy the basis of trust, leaving a landscape of grief, doubt, and confusion. The path to recovery may seem long and difficult, but with dedication, understanding, and a determination to rebuild, it is possible to reassemble the shattered parts and form an even stronger link.

The process starts with admitting the pain produced by the betrayal. The individual who betrayed the trust must accept full responsibility for their actions, demonstrate real regret, and apologize. Equally vital is the damaged partner's willingness to voice their hurt and fury, so that their feelings may be acknowledged and respected.

This healing process relies heavily on open and honest communication. It is about providing a secure environment in which both partners may share their worries, anxieties, and expectations without being judged. This entails carefully listening, asking clarifying questions, and attempting to comprehend each other's views.

Rebuilding trust does not happen immediately; it requires time, patience, and constant effort. It's about proving credibility with deeds rather than just words. The individual who violated the trust must be willing to make apologies, modify their conduct, and continuously present themselves as a dependable and trustworthy partner.

Forgiveness is a valuable tool in the healing process, but it does not mean endorsing the betrayal or ignoring the grief. It is about letting go of the anger and resentment that might keep you from going on. Forgiveness is a personal decision, and it may need time and work to achieve real forgiveness.

Rebuilding trust entails establishing new limits and expectations. This might include improved openness, more regular check-ins, or even couples therapy to address the underlying problems that caused the betrayal. It is critical for both partners to be open about their wants and expectations, and to collaborate to build a fresh foundation of trust.

Chapter 6: The Power of Forgiveness: Healing Wounds and Moving Forward

In the panorama of human emotions, forgiveness shines like a beacon of hope, lighting the route to healing, development, and greater connection. It is a transforming force with the ability to repair broken hearts, rebuild shattered trust, and free us from the bonds of hatred and bitterness. Forgiveness is more than just an act of compassion; it is a purposeful decision to let go of the anguish of the past and embrace the potential of a better future.

At its essence, forgiveness is not about accepting or justifying unpleasant behavior. It is not about ignoring or rejecting the sorrow that has been caused. Rather, it is about admitting the injustice that has been done, letting oneself to experience the whole range of emotions that occur, and eventually deciding to let go of the anger, resentment, and desire for vengeance.

Forgiveness is a gift we offer to ourselves, relieving us of the load of past injuries. When we harbor anger, we become captives of our own suffering, unable to go ahead and accept the pleasure and love that life has to offer. Forgiveness enables us to break away from the cycle of negativity and allow our hearts to heal and regenerate.

The process of forgiving is not always simple or clear. It takes bravery, vulnerability, and a willingness to address our most intense feelings. It may include admitting our grief, expressing our rage and hurt, and seeking understanding and resolution.

One of the first stages toward forgiving is developing empathy and compassion for both ourselves and the person who has wronged us. This does not imply justifying their conduct, but rather attempting to understand the motives and circumstances that led to them. Recognizing that everyone makes errors and is capable of inflicting sorrow allows us to begin to let go of judgment and open our hearts to forgiveness.

Letting go of resentment is an important step in the forgiving process. This entails releasing the bad feelings that have been holding us back, such as rage, resentment, and hate. It entails choosing to concentrate on the present and future rather to linger on the past. It entails acknowledging that harboring animosity only harms ourselves and stops us from going ahead.

Healing and closure may take several forms. It may include communicating freely and honestly with the person who has injured us, expressing our emotions, and requesting an apology. It may also include seeking professional assistance, such as therapy or counseling, in order to process our feelings and establish appropriate coping skills.

Forgiveness is a continuous process that involves patience, understanding, and the desire to let go. It is a journey that may result in deep healing, development, and change. Accepting forgiveness not only frees us from the agony of the past, but it also opens our hearts to the prospect of deeper, more satisfying connections in the future.

The power of forgiveness stems from its potential to alter not just our relationships, but also ourselves. It enables us to let go of the anger and resentment that has been holding us back, and instead embrace love, compassion, and understanding. Forgiving others teaches us to forgive ourselves for our own faults and failings.

In personal relationships, forgiveness is critical for healing scars, restoring trust, and moving ahead together. When we forgive our spouse, we make room for development, understanding, and a stronger bond. We lift the weight of the past and pave the way for a greater future full of love, joy, and lasting satisfaction.

Understanding Forgiveness

Forgiveness, an often-misunderstood notion, does not imply accepting harsh behavior or eliminating the grief caused. It is a purposeful decision to let go of wrath, resentment, and bitterness. It entails admitting the pain, allowing oneself to experience the feelings that come, and then deciding to let go.

Forgiveness does not mean forgetting. The memory of the pain may persist, but its ability to affect your emotions and behaviors decreases. It is about moving your emphasis from the past to the present, from pain to healing. It is acknowledging that hanging onto anger only wounds you, keeping you from progressing and feeling pleasure.

Forgiveness is not a weakness. It takes strength and bravery to face the anguish, own the hurt, and decide to let go. It demonstrates your resilience and devotion to your personal well-being. It's acknowledging that you deserve peace and happiness, and that forgiving is a step toward getting them.

Forgiveness isn't always simple. It may need time, effort, and the desire to address painful feelings. However, the advantages are tremendous. When you forgive, you relieve yourself of the load of wrath and resentment. You allow your heart to heal and make room for love, compassion, and understanding to grow.

Forgiveness isn't just about the other person. This is for you. It's about recovering your power, finding peace, and moving on with your life. It's about choosing to prioritize your own pleasure and well-being above obsessing on the past.

Practical Steps to Forgiveness

Starting along the road of forgiveness is a brave act of self-love and release. It takes a willingness to face uncomfortable emotions, let go of resentment, and accept the potential of healing and progress. While the trip may be difficult, you may take practical actions to help you traverse this transforming process.

Begin by recognizing the grief and hurt created by the transgression. Allow yourself to experience the whole spectrum of feelings that emerge, including anger, grief, and betrayal. Don't ignore or reject your emotions; instead, express them in a healthy manner, such as by writing, talking to a trusted friend, or getting professional treatment.

After you've recognized your suffering, attempt to grasp the viewpoint of the individual who harmed you. This should not imply justifying their actions, but rather attempting to understand their reasons and circumstances. Empathy may be an effective aid in the forgiving process, allowing you to recognize the humanity in the person who has harmed you.

Make the intentional choice to forgive. This is a decision, not a sensation. It may not happen quickly, and you may need to remind yourself of your choice many times. However, by committing to forgiveness, you are setting the intention to let go of the past and move on.

If feasible and appropriate, communicate your forgiveness to the individual who has wronged you. This does not have to be a huge gesture; it may just be a discussion in which you convey your desire to let go of the past and move on. This may be a significant step toward healing for both of you.

Release the desire for vengeance or retribution. Holding onto anger and resentment just keeps you stuck in the past, preventing you from experiencing the pleasure and freedom that forgiveness may provide. Choose to let go of the need to punish or exact retribution, and instead concentrate on your own recovery and well-being.

Concentrate on the present and future. Dwelling on the past and reliving the pain only helps to aggravate the wound. Instead, focus your attention on building a great and satisfying future. Set new objectives, follow your interests, and surround yourself with people that encourage and inspire you.

Chapter 7: Nurturing Individuality

Many people feel that the ultimate objective of a satisfying and long-lasting relationship is to merge into a single entity. However, a really flourishing relationship is about honoring and cultivating your uniqueness within the framework of love, rather than losing yourself in another person. It's about realizing that two entire people coming together may produce a far more lively and dynamic relationship than two halves striving to construct a whole.

Maintaining a sense of self is essential for personal development and relationship fulfillment. It entails respecting your own hobbies, interests, and friendships even when you share your life with another person. It entails being loyal to your values, ideas, and goals while without compromising your identity for the sake of the partnership.

When you accept your uniqueness, you provide a richness and depth to your relationship that cannot be imitated. You share your unique viewpoints, experiences, and abilities with your spouse, enhancing and widening their lives. You also demonstrate the value of self-care and personal development, encouraging your spouse to do the same.

Embracing your distinct hobbies and interests is not only rewarding for you, but also advantageous to the relationship. When you engage in things that make you happy and excited, you exude good energy that carries over into your relationships with your spouse. It maintains the spark and prevents the relationship from becoming stale or monotonous.

Maintaining connections outside of the relationship is also critical for a successful relationship. Your buddies provide a unique combination of support, companionship, and viewpoint. They provide an environment in which you can be yourself, express your problems, and enjoy your accomplishments. Nurturing your friendships helps you avoid being excessively dependent on your spouse for all of your emotional needs, resulting in a more balanced and meaningful existence.

Fostering a loving and encouraging partnership is critical to preserving uniqueness within the relationship. This includes congratulating your spouse on their accomplishments, promoting their personal development, and assisting them in pursuing their own hobbies and interests. It entails being their greatest supporter, being a listening ear, and creating a secure environment for them to express themselves honestly.

When both parties feel supported and encouraged to follow their own paths, the partnership thrives. There is mutual respect, admiration, and appreciation for each other's distinct characteristics and accomplishments. This results in a dynamic and exciting collaboration in which both parties feel satisfied and powerful.

It's crucial to highlight that keeping uniqueness does not imply ignoring the demands of the partnership. It's about striking a good balance between your personal requirements and those of your relationship. It's about discussing freely and honestly about your own aspirations and finding methods to help each other develop while simultaneously nourishing your relationship.

Maintaining a Sense of Self

In the embrace of love, it is easy to lose sight of the unique strands that comprise your beautiful tapestry. However, keeping your own individuality is not only doable, but also required for a really satisfying connection. It's about remembering who you were before the relationship and continuing to develop and improve as a person while sharing your life with someone else.

Your sense of self is an invaluable gift, molded by your experiences, interests, and ideals. It's the essence of who you are, the core that holds true even when life throws you curveballs. Losing contact with this core might make you feel disoriented, unsatisfied, and distant from your own satisfaction.

Preserving your uniqueness in a relationship is not about being selfish or abandoning your spouse; it is about acknowledging that you are two distinct people with different wants and aspirations. It's about establishing an environment in which both of you can thrive, individually and as a pair.

This is setting aside time for things that offer you pleasure and contentment, such as following a hobby, spending time with friends, or just enjoying some peaceful alone. It entails keeping true to your hobbies and interests while prioritizing your relationship.

Maintaining your own thoughts and convictions is just as vital. It is good to have opposing viewpoints and to participate in polite dialogue with your spouse. Don't be hesitant to express your own opinions and emotions, especially if they vary from your partner's. This promotes mutual respect and helps you to learn and develop from each other.

Remember that your spouse loves you for who you are, not who they want you to be. By being loyal to yourself, you not only meet your own needs, but you also enhance the relationship with your own personality and viewpoint. A strong sense of self enables you to contribute your best self to the relationship, resulting in a more lively, gratifying, and long-lasting connection.

So, as you begin on this romantic adventure, remember to nourish the person inside. Embrace your hobbies, appreciate your friendships, and stick to your ideals. You'll not only build an amazing life for yourself, but you'll also help your relationship become stronger, healthier, and more dynamic.

Supporting Each Other's Dreams

Supporting each other's aspirations is a colorful thread in the tapestry of a loving connection, connecting the fabric of mutual respect, encouragement, and steadfast belief. It's about understanding that your partner's goals are not different from your own, but rather an extension of the love and life you share.

When you actively support your partner's goals, you become their greatest cheerleader, confidant, and steadfast source of encouragement. You celebrate their major and little accomplishments while also offering consolation and support amid failures. You listen carefully to their goals and worries, creating a secure environment for them to express themselves truthfully.

Supporting your partner's desires entails more than simply saying encouraging words; it also entails taking concrete steps to assist them in achieving their objectives. It might include providing practical assistance, such as researching resources, connecting them with necessary connections, or just freeing up their time by accepting new duties.

Supporting your partner's aspirations may necessitate making sacrifices. It might include putting your personal goals on wait, altering your schedule, or making financial compromises. Remember that supporting your partner's aspirations is an investment in the future of your relationship. It enhances your tie, deepens your connection, and fosters a common sense of purpose and satisfaction.

When you encourage each other's aspirations, you create an environment in which both partners feel empowered to follow their interests and realize their full potential. You form a team and work together to attain your individual and collective objectives. This generates a feeling of mutual respect, admiration, and appreciation, which strengthens the basis of your relationship.

Chapter 8: Embracing Uniqueness

In the vivid fabric of love, no two people are precisely identical. Each person contributes a distinct set of personality characteristics, interests, and opinions to the relationship, resulting in a rich and diversified terrain of uniqueness. While these differences might cause misunderstandings and conflict, they also have the ability to enhance and strengthen the relationship between spouses.

Embracing individuality in a relationship begins with acknowledging and embracing the natural difference that occurs amongst people. It entails celebrating your partner's unique qualities, quirks, and eccentricities. It entails acknowledging that your differences are not hurdles to be overcome, but rather possibilities for development, learning, and mutual understanding.

Exploring personality types might help you obtain a better grasp of your partner's individuality. While there are other personality frameworks, one popular model is the Myers-Briggs Type Indicator

(MBTI). The MBTI classifies people into 16 personality types based on their preferences for introversion or extroversion, sensing or intuition, thinking or emotion, and evaluating or perceiving. Understanding your partner's personality type may give useful information about their communication style, decision-making process, and general outlook on life.

Recognizing your partner's love language is also a crucial element of knowing their individuality. This notion, promoted by Gary Chapman, proposes that people express and receive love in many forms. The five love languages include words of affirmation, acts of service, getting presents, spending quality time together, and physical contact. Understanding your partner's love language allows you to personalize your demonstrations of affection to their individual requirements, making them feel really appreciated.

Communication styles may also differ greatly between persons. Some individuals are inherently more direct and outspoken, whilst others may be more reserved and oblique. Some people prefer to speak about difficulties right away, while others require time to digest their feelings before sharing them. Understanding your partner's communication style may help you avoid misunderstandings, communicate more effectively, and deal with issues more constructively.

To navigate differences productively, people must be prepared to compromise, talk freely and honestly, and be patient with one another. It entails acknowledging that there is no right or wrong way to be, and that your partner's viewpoint is equally as legitimate as yours. It entails finding methods to appreciate your diversity rather than attempting to shape each other to fit a predetermined pattern.

When conflict emerges due to differences, it is critical to handle the issue with empathy and understanding. Avoid criticizing or condemning your spouse, and instead concentrate on finding solutions that benefit both of you. This might include compromise, negotiation, or just consenting to disagree. Remember that the aim is not to win the debate, but to develop your relationship and find a way to cohabit peacefully despite your differences.

Accepting your partner's individuality may also include learning new things from him or her. If your spouse has a different passion or activity than you, be willing to explore it together. You can find a new passion or get a greater respect for your partner's hobbies. Expanding your horizons together creates opportunity for shared experiences, greater connection, and personal progress.

Understanding Personality Differences

Understanding the interesting realm of personality variations is one of the keys to accepting one's own individuality within a partnership. Each person has a unique collection of characteristics, preferences, and dispositions that influence their thoughts, emotions, and actions. Recognizing and accepting these differences may result in more empathy, compassion, and, eventually, a stronger relationship.

Several personality frameworks, like the Myers-Briggs Type Indicator (MBTI), provide useful insights into these individual differences. Whether you are an introvert or an extrovert, a thinker or a feeler, a judger or a perceiver, knowing your partner's personality type may help you comprehend their communication style, decision-making process, and general attitude to life.

For example, an introvert may like quiet times of introspection, while an extrovert thrives on social engagement and outward stimulation. A thinker may stress logic and reason, while a feeler puts a higher focus on emotions and values. Recognizing these distinctions enables you to communicate more effectively, prevent misunderstandings, and value each other's distinct qualities.

Understanding personality differences does not include classifying or categorizing your spouse; rather, it entails learning more about their inner world and how they live their lives. It's about acknowledging that their way of life is just as legitimate as yours, even if it varies.

When you accept your differences, you make room for mutual respect and admiration. You learn to communicate in ways that are compatible with your partner's personality, and you become more aware of their wants and desires. You also find fresh viewpoints and approaches to life, which enriches your own development.

Learning to Appreciate Each Other's Strengths

Recognizing and appreciating each other's abilities is similar to discovering hidden jewels that bring shine and depth to the relationship. It's about seeing beyond the surface and recognizing the special characteristics that make your relationship sparkle.

When we concentrate on our partner's strengths, we change our view away from what they lack and onto what they give. We come to view them not as a collection of defects and shortcomings, but as a full person with distinct qualities, abilities, and perspectives that enhance our lives.

Appreciating your partner's qualities does not imply dismissing their flaws or struggles. It just involves focusing on the good qualities of their personality and recognizing the value they offer to the partnership. When you show thanks for their abilities, you start a positive feedback loop that promotes those characteristics and stimulates future development.

One strategy to foster appreciation is to make a deliberate effort to identify and appreciate your partner's abilities on a regular basis. It might be as easy as praising them on a job well done, expressing thanks for their assistance, or just telling them how much you love a certain attribute they have.

Another method to recognize your partner's abilities is to discover ways to incorporate them into your relationship. If your spouse is an excellent listener, encourage them to express their ideas and emotions to you. If they are good at issue solving, include them in decision-making processes. Recognizing and exploiting their abilities not only expresses gratitude, but also empowers them to bring their particular gifts to the partnership.

Chapter 9: Building a Life Together

In the journey of love, building shared meaning is the skill of weaving two distinct lives into a cohesive tapestry of hopes, aspirations, and experiences. It is the process of creating a life together, one enhanced by common objectives, treasured traditions, and a deep sense of purpose. Couples who actively participate in generating shared meaning deepen their link while also laying the framework for a future filled with pleasure, contentment, and enduring connection.

Setting common objectives is an essential part of creating a life together. It entails open and honest conversation about individual goals and finding common ground where they overlap. It is about defining common values, objectives, and future goals, and then working together to develop a strategy for attaining them.

These common objectives might vary from personal development and job ambitions to financial stability, travel experiences, and raising a family. The trick is to make both parties feel heard, appreciated, and involved in the process of establishing and achieving these objectives.

Creating shared rituals and customs is another effective strategy to instill significance in your relationship. These routines might be as basic as a weekly date night, a daily coffee routine, or a unique method to commemorate anniversaries and holidays. They may also be more complex, such as yearly vacations, family reunions, or religious ceremonies.

The value of these rituals is not in their intricacy, but in the shared meaning they have for both parties. They provide a feeling of consistency, regularity, and belonging, which strengthens your link and fosters a sense of shared identity. They allow for connection, humor, and intimacy, resulting in enduring experiences that will be treasured for years to come.

Shared experiences provide the foundation of a meaningful life together. They may range from checking out a new restaurant, going to a concert, or exploring a new city together to working on a volunteer project, establishing a company together, or raising a family. These events form a shared history, a collection of tales and memories that bring you together and enhance your bond.

Couples that actively seek out and create shared experiences strengthen their relationship while also expanding their horizons and growing as individuals. They learn new things about one another, uncover hidden abilities and interests, and foster a better feeling of cooperation and collaboration.

Developing common meaning is a continuous process that needs work, communication, and a willingness to compromise. It's about finding methods to integrate your particular aspirations with your joint vision for the future. It is about building rituals and customs that nourish and honor your special relationship. And it's about sharing new experiences together, weaving a tapestry of memories that will last a lifetime.

The benefits of developing shared purpose are immense. It improves the basis of your relationship, deepens your bond, and gives you a feeling of purpose and direction. It provides a common history, a collection of events and memories to reflect on with delight and pride. It also promotes a sense of belonging, a feeling that you are a part of something bigger than yourself, a love that goes beyond the individual and embraces the communal.

Setting Shared Goals

Building a life together requires more than simply shared experiences and customs. It demands a common vision for the future, a set of goals that both partners are dedicated to attaining together. Setting shared objectives is an effective strategy to link your own desires with the collective aims of your relationship.

When you and your spouse sit down to outline your shared objectives, you are effectively building a road map for your future together. This approach includes open and honest discussions about your own wants, goals, and beliefs. It's about finding common ground, establishing intersections between your ambitions, and developing a shared vision that inspires and drives both of you.

These common objectives might vary from personal development and job ambitions to financial stability, travel experiences, and raising a family. The trick is to make both parties feel heard, appreciated, and involved in the process of establishing and achieving these objectives.

Setting shared objectives not only simplifies your vision for the future, but it also enhances your relationship. It promotes a feeling of cooperation, collaboration, and common purpose. When you work together to achieve a shared objective, you learn to communicate more effectively, compromise more easily, and support one another through difficult situations.

The process of accomplishing common objectives may be as enjoyable as the end result. It's about your journey together, the challenges you face, and the lessons you gain along the way. Each milestone you achieve together deepens your relationship and supports your dedication to one another and your common vision for the future.

Cultivating Shared Rituals and Traditions

Shared rituals and traditions serve as anchors at the core of a successful relationship, guiding you and your spouse through a sea of shared events and beloved memories. They are the threads that link the fabric of your own love story, instilling a feeling of belonging, continuity, and delight that strengthens your bond over time.

These rituals might be as basic as a daily good morning kiss, a weekly movie night, or a unique method to mark birthdays and anniversaries. They may also be more complex, such as yearly vacations, family reunions, or religious ceremonies. The idea is to pick rituals that are meaningful to both of you and that you are excited to share together.

The beauty of shared rituals is their capacity to provide stability and comfort in a world that is often chaotic and unexpected. They provide your relationship a feeling of rhythm, structure, and regularity, which can be both grounding and comforting. When you know you have a particular custom to look forward to, it may add an element of excitement and anticipation to your daily life.

Shared rituals provide opportunity for connection, humor, and intimacy. They help you to calm down, block out distractions, and just enjoy each other's presence. Whether it's snuggling up on the sofa for a movie marathon, preparing a dinner together, or going for a stroll in the park, these shared experiences create lasting memories that enhance and deepen your relationship.

Traditions, on the other hand, are practices handed down through generations or created by a pair. They might be cultural, religious, or just personal. Traditions let you connect with your history, heritage, and common beliefs. They create a feeling of continuity and belonging, connecting you to something greater than yourself.

Chapter 10: Maintaining a Healthy Relationship

Love is a never-ending adventure that involves attention, care, and a mutual commitment to progress. Maintaining a good relationship is a continuous process, a lifetime journey full of both pleasures and difficulties. It's about understanding that love is a dynamic energy that demands ongoing attention and care.

A relationship, like a garden, requires continual labor and maintenance in order to develop. It's about putting your spouse first, making time for each other, and engaging in the emotional and physical connection that keeps you together. It is about speaking freely and honestly, resolving issues constructively, and supporting one another's hopes and goals.

One of the most important components of having a successful relationship is accepting change and progress, both individually and as a pair. As individuals, we are always changing, learning, and developing. Our interests, beliefs, and priorities may change over time, and it's critical to make room for this personal development within the framework of the partnership.

Accepting change also entails acknowledging that partnerships are not immune to difficulties and disappointments. Life throws us unexpected curveballs, and how we deal with these problems together reveals the true depth of our relationship. By tackling hardship as a team, talking freely, and supporting one another throughout tough times, we may emerge stronger and more bonded than ever before.

Seeking help and assistance when required demonstrates strength, not weakness. It acknowledges that we do not have all of the answers and that seeking outside assistance may bring significant insights and skills for addressing complicated challenges. Reaching out for help, whether via couples therapy, counseling, or just getting advice from trustworthy friends or family members, may make a significant difference in sustaining a good relationship.

A therapist or counselor may provide a secure and impartial environment for couples to discuss their problems, speak honestly, and develop healthy coping strategies. They may provide advice on communication techniques, conflict resolution solutions, and ways to increase intimacy and connection. Seeking professional treatment is not a sign of failure; rather, it is a proactive move toward developing a deeper and more rewarding relationship.

In addition to obtaining professional help, it is critical to have a strong network of friends and family who can provide encouragement, guidance, and a listening ear. Connecting with people who have had similar issues may bring a feeling of validation and comfort, letting us know that we are not alone in our troubles.

Maintaining a good relationship is an ongoing process of learning, developing, and adjusting. It's about enjoying the good times, overcoming obstacles, and accepting love's ever-changing nature. It's about accepting that the job is never fully finished, but the benefits are immense.

Embracing Change and Growth

Love is not a static snapshot preserved in time. It is a living, breathing organism that changes and develops as we go through life. Accepting the fundamental nature of change and progress, both personally and as a partnership, is essential for sustaining a healthy and satisfying relationship.

As individuals, we are always learning, growing, and finding new aspects of ourselves. Our hobbies, passions, and priorities may change throughout time, and it is important to acknowledge and welcome this personal development within the framework of the partnership. Resisting change or holding onto a fixed vision of yourself or your spouse may hinder progress and lead to stagnation.

Encourage each other to seek new hobbies, set personal objectives, and go out of your comfort zones. Celebrate each other's triumphs, provide support during difficult times, and be open to the potential of change within yourself and your partnership.

Relationships, like people, evolve and change over time. The love you shared at the start of your journey may appear different years later, but it is still genuine and valuable. In fact, recognizing your love's progression may strengthen your relationship and make it even more durable and meaningful.

Remember that change is not to be feared, but rather a chance for development and rejuvenation. It's an opportunity to recapture the flame that lit your love, to explore new levels of intimacy, and to envision a shared future that is even more alive and rewarding than the past.

Conclusion

As we near the conclusion of this transforming voyage into the world of healthy relationships, it's time to reflect on the priceless skills and insights you've received. You've studied the fundamentals of trust, communication, and forgiveness, as well as the power of emotional and physical intimacy. You've also learned how to cherish your differences while creating a shared life full of purpose and meaning.

The route to expressing love is not always straightforward. It needs work, vulnerability, and the resolve to face obstacles front on. However, as you have realized, the benefits are incalculable. A good relationship is a source of pleasure, comfort, and steadfast support, a place where you can be yourself and explore the depths of human connection.

Your adventure does not stop here. The information and abilities you've learned are designed to be used on a regular basis, not kept aside. As you work to strengthen your relationship, keep open communication, active listening, and mutual respect in mind. Accept dispute as a chance for development, and never underestimate forgiveness's ability to heal scars and deepen relationships.

Cultivate shared experiences, develop rituals and traditions with unique value, and encourage one other's hopes and goals. Celebrate your differences, value each other's strengths, and keep learning and developing together.

Remember that developing a long-term connection is an ongoing process. It demands consistent work, dedication, and a desire to adapt and change. But with the strategies you've learned from this book, you'll be well-prepared to face the inevitable hurdles and cultivate a love that grows over time.

As you begin the next chapter of your journey, may you continue to harness the power of good connections in your life. May your love be a source of pleasure, inspiration, and constant support, demonstrating the everlasting power of the human heart to connect, heal, and flourish.